PRISONER FOR CHRIST

Other books by Stanley Maxwell

The Man Who Couldn't Be Killed

The Man Who Lived Twice

How God sustained Pastor Huang
in a Shanghai prison

PRISONER FOR CHRIST

STANLEY MAXWELL
based on a story told by
ROBERT HUANG

Pacific Press® Publishing Association
Nampa, Idaho
Oshawa, Ontario, Canada
www.pacificpress.com

Designed by Dennis Ferree
Cover photo by SW Productions/Getty Images ©

Additional copies of this book are available by calling toll free 1-800-765-6955 or
by visiting http://www.adventistbookcenter.com.

Library of Congress Cataloging-in-Publication-Data

Maxwell, Stanley M., 1958-
Prisoner for Christ : how God sustained Pastor Huang in a Shanghai prison/
Stanley Maxwell; based on a story told by Robert Huang.
p. cm.
ISBN: 0-8163-2054-3
1. Huang, Robert. 2. Seventh-day Adventists—China—Shanghai—Clergy—
Biography. 3. Persecution—China—History—20th century. 4. China—Politics and
government—1949- I. Huang, Robert. II. Title.

BX6193.H83M39 2004
286.7'092—dc22
[B]
2004040004

03 04 05 06 07 • 5 4 3 2 1

Dedicated to:

My Grandpa ("Uncle Arthur"),
Mom, Dad ("Uncle Mervyn"),
Mary Huang, because there is something about Mary,
Phemie and the Gong family (known as "Mr. Wong's" family in
The Man Who Couldn't Be Killed).

Contents

Preface

When my father, Dr. C. Mervyn Maxwell, taught church history at Andrews University in the 1970s, he used an adage that became quite well known at the time: "A little persecution strengthens the church, too much destroys it." Using his background in early church history, he showed that the pagan persecution of the Christians in Roman times helped the church to grow because, as Tertullian wrote, "the blood of the martyrs is seed."

My father told his seminarians that the situation in Communist China (as it was then called) illustrated how too much persecution destroys the church. A man who loved primary sources, he required his students to read a letter that had been smuggled to the West. It was written in China by the de facto leader of the Adventist Church in Shanghai, David Lin.

In his widely circulated letter, David Lin explained why the Adventists lost China: too much emphasis on institutionalism and not enough effort to ground the workers in Adventism. Later, after China and Vietnam fell to Communism, Dr. Gottfried Oosterwal wrote an article for *Spectrum* magazine, in which he questioned the whole philosophy of sending missionaries overseas. From the standpoint of Adventist history, these documents mark the death knell to the long-standing system of church missions in the Adventist world. While the church at large struggled to find solutions to the problems cited in these sources, Christians in China suffered.

The Christians in Shanghai were cut off from the rest of the world and persecuted by the government until, for a time, the church as an institution ceased to exist. During this traumatic period, Robert Huang (pronounced "hwong") was able to work as an underground pastor in Shanghai long after most of the other Adventist pastors had been incarcerated or, after apostatizing, had become Party collaborators. In time he was placed in a notorious prison in Shanghai, where his faith was tried to its limits. What Robert Huang saw and heard as the institutionalized church became a church of individuals is described in this book. His story shows how he encouraged those individuals to remain faithful.

The characters in this book are real. This book is derived from a true story, the facts drawn from hundreds of pages of primary sources written by Robert Huang, archival research, two trips to China, interviews with Robert Huang, and investigations of actual sites. I ran across some of the material used here serendipitously while researching for my master's degree in history at Andrews University. Some names have been changed to protect the innocent—or the guilty, as the case may be. The scholarly reader might be interested to know that Dr. Huang was issued more prison numbers than those given here.

My sincere thanks go to some who helped in the writing of this opus, especially to Dr. Robert Huang for giving me the opportunity to write his story; Jerry Thomas and Tim Lale for challenging and encouraging me to undertake the project; Dr. Bruce Closser for literary advice; S. Lawrence Maxwell, Debi Everhart, and Dr. Ron du Preez for proofreading and editing; Dr. C. Mervyn Maxwell and Dr. Ron du Preez for their wise counsel; my wife, Phemie, for translating during interviews with Mary, and last, but not least, my mother, Pauline G. Maxwell, and the staff at the Ellen G. White Estate for providing archival documents related to the Accusation Movement.

Stanley Maxwell
Osh, Kyrgyzstan
August 2003

Foreword

A note from Robert Huang in his own words:

I wanted to entitle this book *All the Way My Savior Leads Me,* because the sentiment of this favorite song of mine has been the theme that has echoed throughout my life.

I remember in 1972, the first time I stepped into my home in Shanghai after eight years of separation, when the family was gathered around, I suggested right away, "Shall we sing together hymn number 153?" (in the Chinese hymn book). Even now I still love it very much. Often when I sing it to myself or with the congregation, my eyes fill with grateful tears, and I am sure it will be my song through endless ages, for Jesus still leads me all the way.

Fanny J. Crosby, blinded at nine months of age, acknowledged through her long life that,

> All the way my Savior leads me;
> What have I to ask beside?
> Can I doubt His tender mercy,
> Who through life has been my guide?

How can I not say a hearty "Amen!" since God's love, mercy, grace, and wonderful guidance have been so clearly revealed and mingled in my life?

PRISONER FOR CHRIST

After I shared my story in public, many of our church members, teachers, and schoolmates here and there urged me to write something in more detail about my experience. I am well aware of my poor English. They also recognized the problem, but still they not only encouraged me to do it but actively helped me with this writing. I am very much indebted to them and really appreciate these dear brethren and sisters in Christ, for they have helped me in the correction and typing of this manuscript. For certain reasons, I won't mention their names here. God knows them, and so do I. I would especially like to thank Stanley Maxwell, my co-author, for all his help editing and rewriting the text.

I wish to dedicate this small book to all my beloved Christian friends and coworkers in our Lord; also to my lovely family members whom I have mentioned in my story, telling of their concerns for me, and how they comforted me and suffered with me in my long trial.

I recall one renowned Chinese writer who once said that people usually pay more attention to and are more curious about two kinds of people—soldiers and prisoners. This can be easily understood, because in general the people themselves lack such an experience and knowledge. By spiritual implication—once I was a prisoner as well as a soldier of the Lord.

So, of course, I will gladly write and share with them in a little more detail the events of my past. But the main reason for writing my story is that I do not write merely to satisfy curiosity; on the contrary, I feel that if, in writing this tome, I fail to testify of God's love, mercy, justice, chastisement, and power in my life, or in the history of the Chinese church so that people may better know God, Satan, themselves and mankind, this project would be a worthless task.

I am only a little one of God's children whom He has received and treated so tenderly and so amazingly. I am a voice in the wilderness, sounding out in these last days:

All glory to our God and my Savior!

Robert Huang
Tennessee

Introduction

I always enjoy eating in restaurants. Many such meals have been memorable, but very few top the dinner in the Panda Hotel in Tsuen Wan off the coast of Hong Kong when it was still a British colony. The restaurant was famous for its fresh fish that swam in aquariums that lined the walls. Diners would select a fish, which would be caught, cooked, and served. According to the tradition, the fish had been pre-pared properly if its gills were still moving.

Across from me sat Mei-Mei, daughter of Mr. Gong, widely known as Mr. Wong in my book, *The Man Who Couldn't Be Killed.* Beside her sat her husband and her teenage children. They were chatting in Cantonese with my wife, Phemie. Sitting beside me, where I could talk to him in English, was Dr. Robert Huang (pronounced "hwong"), the hero of this book and no relation to "Mr. Wong." We joked about the confusion that the similarity of the names of the two men had caused. Dr. Huang was the underground pastor known in my first book as Charlie Chu, who visited the Gong children in the hospital the day that Mr. Wong's son Lee died.

Besides friendship, there were two purposes for the meal that evening. One was obvious, while the other was more subtle. My wife and I were celebrating the publication of my book, which was just hot off the press. I hoped, also, to persuade Dr. Huang to let me

write the story of his faith and courage under Communist persecution in the days of Chairman Mao. Dr. Huang had served as an
underground pastor in Shanghai after the institutional church collapsed. He claimed to have been the last pastor arrested for proselytizing in the city. For preaching the gospel, he served more than
eight years behind bars. Dr. Huang's story details the struggles of
one Chinese family who lived through that period and how they
held on to their belief in God.

After I had autographed copies of *The Man Who Couldn't Be
Killed* and presented them as gifts, Dr. Huang asked me what I had
been doing lately. I told him that when I wasn't teaching English in a
government college, I was finishing my second book, which was about
an Adventist in Vietnam. I was thinking of calling it *The Man Who
Lived Twice* and hoped it would be published soon.

"Ah," he said. "Did you know my story has been published?"

Suddenly nervous, I asked, "Who published it?"

"The Adventist publishing house in Korea liked my story so much,
they translated it into Korean." He laughed unhappily. "So sad." He
shook his head. "Koreans can read it, but Chinese cannot."

I asked, "Has it been published in English?"

He sighed. "No. I send to major Christian publishers. They say to
me, 'If the Sabbath were not in the story, I would print it.' " He sighed
again. "Sometimes I wish I could leave the Sabbath out, but I cannot."

I suggested that Pacific Press in the United States might like it.
"They think the Sabbath makes stories more interesting." I added.

"That's true," he agreed.

I asked, "Do you still have the manuscript?"

"Yes," he said. "I keep a copy."

"If you like," I said, "I can adapt an Asian story so Western people
can understand it, and I think I can get it published. Would you like
me to write your story my way?"

That was the key question. I had cast the line. What would it reel
in?

After considerable thought, he said, "You write about Vietnam now."

Clearly he was not ready to trust me with his story. Heeding my
wife's advice (she grew up in Hong Kong), I did not press the matter
but switched the conversation to other things.

Introduction

A year went by. *The Man Who Lived Twice* was finished and appeared on the shelves. I was looking for another hero to write about. If only Dr. Huang would let me write about him!

One sunny morning as I walked down the hill to my apartment in Tsuen Wan, I noticed Dr. Robert Huang on the other side of the street coming up toward his apartment. When he neared me, he turned abruptly, crossed the street, and held out a manila envelope. "Read this," he said. "It has blessed many people." Handing me his business card, he pointed: "This is my home phone. When you finish reading, call me." Without waiting for an answer, he turned and marched quickly on up the hill.

Wherever I had been going a few minutes before was no longer important. Not with that envelope in my hand! Rushing to my apartment, I sat on a bench in the courtyard and pored over the manuscript.

Once I felt somewhat familiar with the story, I dialed Dr. Huang's number. After talking pleasantries, I said, "I've never heard you tell your story. People say you tell it very well."

"How do you like my book?" he asked.

"Fascinating in places," I replied, "and dreadfully confusing in others. I have problems with the time line. If I hear you tell your story from beginning to end, it will become clear to me."

"Come on over," he said, and we made an appointment.

So began a string of conversations and long-distance phone calls. The more I wrote about Dr. Robert Huang, this faithful Adventist pastor who suffered so much in the cruel prisons of Shanghai, the more I respected him.

As you read his story, you'll see why.

CHAPTER 1

Students Close Down Schools

Robert Huang looked shorter and stockier than most people in his hometown of Shanghai because his ancestors were from Canton province in southern China. He was, however, blessed with the fair complexion for which the Shanghainese are famed. His thick black horn-rimmed glasses, which seemed too big for his nose, made him look every bit a scholar—even though he was only a fourteen-year-old high school student.

It was an important day for Robert. Looking down suddenly at his watch, he knew that he had to hurry. He didn't want to be late! Hurriedly, he rushed down the three flights of wooden stairs that led from his mother's apartment to the street.

Dashing down Shanghai's bustling streets toward the Seventh-day Adventist church near his home, Robert pondered what the seminary students from Nanjing were planning to do. They had summoned an assembly at the church, which meant that the number expected to attend was far greater than would fit into his high-school auditorium. What exactly did they have in mind?

It was November 1951, two years after Communist Party chairman Mao Zedong had triumphantly liberated free-wheeling Shanghai and chased Chinese Nationalist president Chiang Kai-shek to the island of Taiwan. There Chiang had set up his fledgling government of the

PRISONER FOR CHRIST

Republic of China. The rest of the world would debate for decades the question of who had lost China. Meanwhile, for the average citizen, life in the Chinese mainland carried on almost as usual. However, the spirit of revolution hung in the air.

Thinking about the posters he had read, Robert was sure that Christian schools were about to be closed indefinitely all across China, starting with the little Adventist school he had been attending. This is not to say that the student action would change anything at his school. It surely wouldn't. In light of all the turmoil, though the academic year had not been completed, classes at his Adventist academy had already been cancelled. The announcement at the assembly would only make a de facto situation official. He felt certain that after Christian schools were shut down, it would be only a matter of time before all schools in China would be closed. Shaking his head, Robert sighed as he wondered, *What will be the fate of my generation without education?*

Analyzing the situation, Robert concluded that for the first few years after the Communist liberation of China in 1949, the new leaders had been more interested in crushing capitalism and replacing it with socialism than in dealing with religion and education. Now that policy had changed. Because Robert's school was a Christian school, shutting it down would be a strike at both religion and education. Under the old policy, the government in free-wheeling Shanghai had had its hands full reforming capitalism and corruption (these words were synonymous to Communists). Before World War II, the city of Shanghai had more than a dozen national flags and autonomous sections. Each section was ruled by a different colonial power. A person actually needed many visas just to walk from one side of the city to another. Capitalists, gangsters, and *compradors*[1] flourished. To China's new government officials, these were all evil elements to be rooted out. Consequently, after 1949, China's economic freedoms were marooned on the islands of Taiwan and Hong Kong and on the Macao peninsula, while Chinese on the mainland were punished for being successful businessmen and wealthy landlords.

At that time, Christianity in the Chinese mainland was left alone by the authorities and had even been permitted to flourish. In fact, it was after Liberation in 1949 that Robert Huang attended Seventh-day

Students Close Down Schools

Adventist evangelistic meetings conducted in the city. Hearing the message then eventually led to his being baptized.

Robert's baptism had been delayed almost a year. Most schools in China conducted classes six days a week, from Monday through Saturday, so Robert had had Sabbath problems at his Catholic school. His pastor informed him that he could not join the Adventist church until he was celebrating the Sabbath every week. Unable to resolve the situation at his Catholic school, Robert transferred the next semester to the Adventist academy on Ningkuo Road, a five-day school. He was baptized on August 26, 1950.

Not long afterward, tragedy struck his family. Both his grandfather and his father died in the same year. His grandfather was 90, but his father died at only 42—of tuberculosis complicated by a needless operation. Robert considered it his baptism by fire. But his fiery immersion had only just begun.

As soon as the leaders of the Chinese government thought they had successfully established socialism and reformed corruption, they began to eliminate Christianity. Their strategy was to control it and cut off its foreign support. Soon rumors spread about the coming of an "Accusation Movement." Beijing wanted to weed out bad elements in the churches. All churches in China were to be involved, but, at the last minute, the Catholics and Christians (as Protestants are called in China) persuaded the government to allow the Adventist "cult" to have the "privilege" of spearheading the movement. The Communists agreed because they feared the rapid spread of Adventism after Liberation. Catholics and Protestants encouraged the Adventist students in their task of pioneering the Accusation Movement near Nanjing because they hated Adventists for "stealing sheep" from their congregations. At first, nobody in Shanghai knew exactly what the Accusation Movement was. Indeed, Nanjing found out sooner than anticipated. For many Adventist church leaders, this grass-roots movement was far worse than anything they had ever expected.

News reached Shanghai that some students at the Adventist seminary near Nanjing had, with the government's blessing, called an assembly, during which they accused the missionaries, teachers, and administrators of wrongdoing. As a result, the school was shut down so that students could form committees to continue the Accusation

Movement. The ultimate goal of these so-called Adventist students, with the government's blessing, was to eliminate Christianity from China—beginning with the Adventists. Almost immediately, the more active students traveled by train to the Adventist academies in Shanghai to form new "Accusation Committees" there. The news of their arrival virtually paralyzed Shanghai's Adventist schools.

Soon, as Robert recalled, communiqués from the Accusation Movement were being delivered in the Adventist schools and churches, along with the many other political announcements that were then being read at Seventh-day Adventist worship services. He saw signs nailed to bulletin boards in the streets and posts around the city announcing that the Adventist school Robert attended would be shut down by the seminary students from Nanjing. The announcement called for all students and faculty to attend an assembly at the Adventist church.

Robert had listened to the announcements and had stopped to read the propaganda after school. He'd decided that it would be foolish not to attend. It was better to go willingly than to be forced. Besides, he'd reasoned, he needed to learn about the new Communist regime.

The assembly had been called at the church because the academy facilities were inadequate to hold all who had been invited. Everyone knew that after the students from the Adventist seminary had organized accusation meetings on their campus in Nanjing, school there had been canceled. One unfortunate teacher had been arrested as a spy for the Kuomintang, the unlucky army that the Communists had forced to flee to Taiwan from China. Shanghainese also knew that the faculty and administrators at the seminary had cooperated with the students. The seminary teachers had known who was supporting the students—the central authorities in Beijing. Robert foresaw that his generation would deprive themselves of a valued commodity—education.

Entering the church, Robert sat down in a middle row. Bright red Communist flags were displayed prominently. Banners written in large Chinese characters decorated the walls. They boldly declared the hypocrisy of Christianity and pointed to the "faults"—both real and imagined—of the foreign missionaries, focusing upon the "corruption"—some real and some presumed—among the church administrators. On the platform, a government officer clad in a blue Mao suit sat beside an Adventist church leader. Seated on either side of them were some of the students from Nanjing.

Robert hoped that, in his location in a middle pew, he would be unnoticed. Being a teenager was a decided advantage. He was possibly the youngest member of the local church. The government, in its revolutionary zeal, seemed mostly concerned with the elderly. Perhaps, Robert thought, if he attracted no attention to himself he would seem insignificant. He had already determined to take no part in the Accusation Movement. "Judge not, lest ye be judged," said the Holy Scripture. It didn't seem reasonable to Robert that God would set up Christians to be accusers. That was the work of the evil one.

Robert's thoughts were interrupted when one of the students from Nanjing climbed onto the platform. Stepping up to the microphone, he shouted, "School will be closed for the Accusation Movement. We have important business to conduct. It is our responsibility to weed out bad elements in our society before they destroy China!" No one made a sound as the student sat back down in the congregation.

Another student arose, stepped to the microphone and yelled, "The foreign missionaries are American spies who encourage Chinese to break China's laws!"

The statement rekindled Chinese xenophobia. Almost immediately a majority of the members united against a common enemy—*wai-gwo ren*—"outsiders." Many in the assembly stood up and shouted, "The missionaries are running dogs for the Western imperialists! They help the West keep China down. Down with the missionaries!"

Robert looked carefully around and sighed with relief. The few missionaries who had not left China after the Communist takeover in 1949 had chosen not to attend.

Many students and church members rose to condemn the missionaries. Some accused them of committing crimes, especially espionage. Others described how missionaries, whom they named, had treated Chinese unequally and unjustly. Some others denounced Adventism because it relied so heavily upon the writings of Ellen G. White, who they said was an American spy.

At this point Robert knew he was potentially vulnerable. He could be selected for questioning, because, to many, he was not purely Chinese. They called him *wai kiu* (pronounced "why Q"), or "foreign Chinese." Although he was born in Shanghai, his father and his grandfather were *not* Shanghainese but Cantonese; therefore, as far as the city inhabitants were concerned, he was not really Shanghainese. Being of Cantonese descent made him an outsider of sorts. The Cantonese have a different mentality from the Shanghainese, and the Cantonese dialect is almost a different language from Shanghainese.

Robert realized that his Cantonese background was not the only problem. His peasant-born grandfather had, after losing his crops in a devastating flood, emigrated from Canton Province to San Francisco in the late 1800s. In California he had married an attractive Chinese émigré. After scrimping and saving while working for a butcher, Robert's grandfather had opened a grocery store. Besides selling produce, he and his wife produced a large family with many sons. Robert's father had been born in Watsonville, California, in 1908. When he retired, Robert's grandfather, by then a relatively wealthy man, had returned to his motherland along with his oldest son, Robert's father. Rather than returning to Canton, they had settled in Shanghai. His father married a local beauty, and soon a little family grew. As a result, Robert, in addition to being a Cantonese living in Shanghai, was also the son of an American-born Chinese with uncles still living in the United States. Robert himself had held an American passport until 1950, when it had expired. America, after severing ties with Beijing when China fell to Communism in 1949, had moved its consulate from Shanghai to Taiwan soon afterward. With no American embassy in mainland China, Robert could not have gotten his American passport reissued, even if he'd wanted to.

Though he was no longer an American citizen, to those around him Robert was not totally Chinese, but *wai kiu*, an "overseas Chinese." To them, his heritage inferred that his sphere of thought was not absolutely traditional. He was suspect because he would be more open to new ideas. His having a "Western mentality" made him impure and untrustworthy. He had to admit that, though this distinction might be considered unfair, it often worked to his advantage. China is customarily softer in its treatment toward outsiders than toward insiders. His status as *wai kiu* had often spared him from trouble he might have encountered otherwise. But, as he sat listening to church members accuse foreigners of wrong-doings, Robert knew the winds could turn against him. He too could be accused of espionage.

Before he could worry too much, a government official took the microphone and read a prepared statement from a well-known Adventist leader. In it, the church leader confessed to many crimes against the Communist government.[2]

Soon the church no longer sounded like a house of prayer, for pandemonium broke out. Many in the assembly stood and denounced others in the congregation. Wives accused husbands, and husbands accused wives. Children criticized their parents, and parents betrayed their children.

A church member screamed, "Our church administrators were educated in America, so they think like foreigners. Their loyalty to China is suspect!"

Someone in the audience noticed that one of the church administrators, whose name was Vast Ocean Chu, was conspicuously silent. He was brought forward, forced to stand on the platform, and ordered to hang his head in submission, which he did. The students focused their energies upon Mr. Chu, shouting, "How can you be a Christian when you know about the terrible crimes the missionaries have committed?"

Robert sat up in his chair. *How will Vast Ocean Chu respond?* he asked himself.

Mr. Chu replied, "While I cannot defend all the actions of the missionaries, I cannot say that their crimes against China indicate that Christianity is wrong." Robert noticed that, though Vast Ocean's head remained down, his tone was not submissive; and his answer was instructive. Chu had agreed with the accusers without compromising his principles.

Aggravated by Chu's answer, one of the students shouted, "One of the missionaries had a gun!"

Again Vast Ocean replied calmly. "If it's a crime to own a gun, and if that missionary owned one, he broke the law and should be punished."

Smiles spread across the students' faces. "Don't you see that Christianity is anti-Party and counterrevolutionary? Renounce it as bourgeois liberalism and join the Accusation Movement, or you'll be responsible for the consequences!"

"Just because a missionary owned a gun doesn't alter my faith in God," Chu replied bravely. "Christians make mistakes, and they will pay the consequences. I don't decide whether my religion is right or wrong by looking at church members—even if they are foreigners! I look to Jesus as the author and finisher of my faith."

"If you believe their lies about Jesus, you're a running dog for the imperialists," the students shouted. "Get off your horse, open your eyes, and see what they've done. America is attacking our comrades in Korea.[3] The missionaries have softened you up with Christianity so that their governments can crush us under imperialism!" Clearly, the leaders of the Accusation Movement were dissatisfied with Chu's answers. When they saw that he would not alter his position, they presented new evidence against him, urging him to admit that Christianity was a Western religion imposed upon the Chinese by the evil imperialists to suppress them.

In reply to each new accusation, Vast Ocean humbly maintained an outwardly submissive attitude. Yet, while never denying that individual missionaries might have committed crimes against the Chinese people, or that others might have worked closely with their own governments to betray China, he insisted that their misdeeds did not prove that Christianity was wrong. Chu concluded, "Christ has already paid the penalty for their crimes so that they can be forgiven if they would only ask Jesus and accept Him as the Lord of their lives."

"Then you confess that some Christians have betrayed China," the students concluded. "Tell us their names!" Vast Ocean couldn't think of any names. The students pulled out their trump card. "Admit that you support counterrevolutionary elements who wish to betray China!"

Mr. Chu claimed he was unaware of supporting any counterrevolutionaries. The students urged him to confess, saying, "We know what you've done. Confess, and your punishment will be lighter!" Chu requested an explanation.

A toothy smile spread across one student's face. He sneered, "You hired a Kuomintang spy who sought to overthrow the People's government!" The student approached Vast Ocean. Standing inches from Mr. Chu's face, he declared, "You remember what happened to that spy?"

Chu hung his head lower. "The People caught him. He was tried, convicted, and hanged."

"Then you admit you support bad elements who aim to harm the People's government?" the student shouted victoriously.

"Though I was unaware of his intentions when I hired him, he turned out to be anti-Party, which reflects badly on me," Vast Ocean replied. "My religion teaches me to respect my government. In that light, I can assure you I'll be more careful when I select staff in future."

"Then you confess to hiring a spy?"

"I hired a man who was hanged for spying. I take responsibility for that."

Ecstatic that they had secured a confession of sorts out of Vast Ocean Chu, the student leaders allowed him to return to the congregation, but not without warning him that he would be required to revise his story. "The merciful People's government will grant you another opportunity to confess and repent."

Soon the Nanjing students and Beijing cadres[4] officially closed down the school, and the meeting was adjourned, but not before groups were organized to continue the Accusation Movement. Slowly the assembly spilled out the church door and onto Shanghai's busy streets.

As Robert walked home, he thanked God that he had not been singled out for questioning. With each step, he reviewed the events of the afternoon. His keen sense of right and wrong, based on earlier Bible studies, obliged him to disagree with many of the postulates put forth at the assembly. He knew he harbored no ill will toward the missionaries. No missionary with whom he had become acquainted had tried to undermine China. All of them had come to Shanghai out of love for fellow human beings and out of an earnest desire to share the Gospel with Chinese. *After all,* Robert remembered, *a missionary evangelist taught me about the Bible.*

Robert was certain that in the church that day he had observed the fulfillment of prophecy taught by American missionaries. His heart reached out to the administrator who had shamed himself by publicly renouncing his religion. The prophet had foretold that many great lights would go out in the last days. This was the persecution that marked the time of the end. Would the Chinese church be able to withstand? Robert wondered if he himself would be able to stand.

Who would be next? Vast Ocean Chu had valiantly remained firm under persecution, and Robert admired his diplomatic answers.

Grateful that he had not been chosen to join a group in which to continue the Accusation Movement, Robert determined to have nothing further to do with it. As far as he was concerned, accusing the brethren was the devil's work.

In the following days Robert heard that other meetings were called. The students from Nanjing joined with the hospital and press employees in Shanghai and made plans to accuse the administrators in the hospital and in the publishing house. No one seemed to notice that Robert attended none of the assemblies. Had he showed up for the meeting at the press, he learned later, he would have seen the employees publicly denounce Adventism by defiantly puffing on cigarettes, an Adventist taboo.

The Accusation Movement shut down many Adventist institutions in Shanghai, much to the satisfaction of the disgruntled forces within institutionalized Adventism as well as of the Communist government, the Catholics, and the Protestants. It also necessitated the departure of the remaining foreign missionaries from China.

It was indeed a dark time for Chinese Christianity in general, and for the Shanghainese Seventh-day Adventist Church in particular. Sadly, as history would later reveal, this was not the end of troubles for Christians in China. As Robert himself would soon find out, it was only the beginning.

---

[1] *Comprador:* A foreigner, usually from India or the Near East, who served as an intermediary between the Chinese merchants and the British taipans. A taipan is a great merchant, usually the head of a foreign house in China.

[2] Much later, after the Accusation Movement against the Adventists was over, the leader would claim that the official had edited the statement and had him making statements that he never made; he also would claim that the letter did not reflect his true sentiments because it had been written under duress.

[3] The Accusation Movement took place during the Korean War. China supported the North Korean regime. When Americans shot down Chinese who had come to the aid of their North Korean compatriots, China panicked and struck out against anything American.

[4] According to *The Oxford Encyclopaedic Dictionary of English*, ed, Joyce M. Hawkins and Robert Allen (New York: Oxford University Press, 1991), a *cadre*, pronounced "kader," is a group of activists in a communist or any revolutionary party; a member of such a group. Often, in post-Mao China, a *cadre* is a government official of some rank.

CHAPTER 2

Up on the Roof, Praying

It was Robert's senior year. Since the Accusation Movement had successfully closed down his academy the previous school year, Robert had had no alternative but to attend a public high school. Students were rarely allowed to transfer to another high school in the last year of their program. To make matters worse, such transfers were unheard-of among applicants, like Robert, who had attended a Christian school. Nevertheless, after praying for God's guidance, he had applied.

After he was accepted, he knew that some people might have said to him, "Perhaps it was because you are a *wai kiu* (outsider)." Possibly others could have claimed it was "due to the new society formed under Liberated Shanghai." In general, everyone thought that when China started down the socialist road, everything would improve for the average person. Robert thought there was another explanation. When the news arrived, he believed it was nothing less than an answer to prayer. Many students wishing to transfer had long waits. This was especially the case for candidates from Christian schools. Making matters worse, the Adventist academy he had attended had not been accredited, which should have made a transfer even more difficult. But what amazed Robert the most was that he had been allowed to start classes in the new school—a prestigious high school in his district—without having to take a break in his educational program.

Soon he found himself accepted in more ways than one. Despite the fact that he was a new student in his final year, he was chosen to serve as a cadre for his class. This position afforded him leadership opportunities. Being a cadre granted him the possibility of becoming a Communist Youth League member—with all its privileges and potential for advancement into Party membership. He also maintained high marks for his school work, which naturally pleased his teachers.

Unfortunately, not everything was rosy. Offsetting his blessings was one major pitfall. School met Monday through Saturday. Robert decided to spend Saturday with God. Every Friday he requested Saturday off to attend church. At first, his teachers were very understanding. As long as he made up his homework, they didn't mind if he missed a day. On his part, Robert never failed to turn in his homework for Saturday. He conscientiously asked students to tell him what assignments he had missed and to explain what the teacher taught in class. Sunday, when many students were playing, he was always studying.

The trouble began while Robert was simply sitting in class. Miss Woo Lan, the vice dean, opened the classroom door and interrupted the teacher by announcing, "I want to see Robert Huang in my office now."

Puzzled and slightly embarrassed, Robert followed Vice Dean Woo down the hall to her office. Inside, they sat down. "We're very proud of you, Robert."

Robert looked down bashfully to deflect the praise.

"You're a good student. Your marks are high and you're a school cadre."

"It is nothing," Robert replied humbly. "Nothing."

"You could have a bright future in New China." Then Vice Dean Woo came to the point. "Because you're so young, Robert, you must understand that in our country, for the religious people there is no future. *Ni mae yo banfa!* You have no path to follow! So I think you'd better give up your religion like I did." She laughed nervously. "You see, I was a Catholic, so I have some understanding of religion. When I saw I had no future if I continued to worship God, I just gave it up. I'm concerned about you, Robert. You're a student with such promise. I'd like to see you meet your potential, so I just give you this little advice, huh? Please, learn from my experience."

"Thank you for your sincerity," Robert answered. "You're a good teacher, and you're very kind to take your time to talk to me about so serious a problem." Then he decided to leave her a testimony: "I cannot give up my faith."

"You think about this seriously, Robert. This is my good will to you because you're a cadre and a good student." With that, she told Robert, "Return to your classroom now."

Robert hoped that their little discussion would be the end of the matter, but it turned out not to be. Friday, following school regulations, he filled out a request for Saturday off to worship God. The permission was denied, as he had expected, based on his experience. While his teachers may have been somewhat understanding, the administrators were not. Undeterred, he attended church anyway. On Sunday, he asked students for help with his assignments and completed Saturday's homework. Monday, when he returned to school, he sat in a routine assembly. Generally, the announcements read by the dean were lengthy and boring. But announcements would never again be boring for Robert; they would become a source of increasing tension. On that particular Monday, Robert heard his name mentioned and pricked up his ears. After the dean had exhorted the students to study hard and get good grades and had urged them to be loyal to Chairman Mao and follow the socialist path, he told the students to be "cautious about the Sabbath. Don't follow the example of Robert Huang. There is no excuse for truancy. Education and the socialist way must always precede superstition!"

After one of his classes, a couple of his classmates approached him in the hall. "We're concerned about your future," one said. "You're so young. Why so superstitious? Why insist upon this kind of tradition? Why not follow the socialist path?"

In the days that followed, other students walked him home from school, earnestly trying to help him see the follies of religion. They gave him books, which he read to understand how they thought. One was entitled, *Niu Mang*, or *Gadfly*, and was very popular in Shanghai at the time. A movie based on the story was shown in Chinese theatres. It told the story of a Catholic bishop in Europe who learned that his illegitimate son (whom he'd never claimed and who was to-tally ignorant as to who his father was) had joined the revolutionaries and, in so doing, had betrayed his Catholic country. The bishop re-ported his son to the authorities, even though he knew it would mean capital punishment. The son was tried and condemned to death. Then, in a twist of fate, the bishop was assigned to labor for the traitor's soul before his execution. The authorities had no idea about the true rela-tionship between the "Judas" and his designated priest. In the cell, the bishop unwittingly displayed his mixed feelings for the prisoner. He tried to lead him to God but failed. When the condemned man learned that the bishop was his father and that he was the one who had turned him in to the government, tension mounted. The pris-oner declared, "Even though I stand at death's door, I will never ac-cept Catholicism." The desperate father cried, pleading with his son, to no avail. The young man, unable to synchronize the bishop's behav-ior with his beliefs, hated him. He died proudly defiant.

When the students learned that Robert had read the book, they told him, "The story clearly illustrates that Christians cannot be trusted. Religious people are hypocrites. They cannot stand in society. Their superstition blocks progress. It's better to learn socialism, because those who follow the socialist path are dependable. If we all journey down the same road, it will lead us to a perfect society under Communism, where everybody will pull their own weight based on their abilities."

Robert replied, "In reading this book, I learned a little bit about the Catholic Church. In past centuries, they have traditionally involved themselves in politics. So, for this reason, I say, 'The Catholic Church and our church, our faith, my religion, the Seventh-day Adventist Church, are different. Unlike the Catholics, we Adventists separate ourselves from national politics. So, this kind of thing—I mean the story of the bishop and his illegitimate son—will never happen in my church.' " His classmates were incredulous.

Thinking back, when Robert considered the story of the traitor and the bishop, he remembered sitting in the auditorium during the Accusation Movement. Seeing similarities, he reminded himself that, like Vast Ocean Chu, he should not look to people but to Christ for his example, and that he should read the Bible, not stories of the failings of men, for a true understanding of the Christian way. Sadly, whenever he tried to explain these thoughts to his classmates, the testimony fell on rocky soil and never sprouted. Instead, the pressure to bend mounted continuously, until Robert feared he was at a breaking point. Clearly there were two paths to guide him. The road he'd chosen was becoming increasingly difficult.

"Robert Huang!"

The sound of his name rudely awakened him to reality. "You were absent again." Robert did not listen to the rest of the statement. Vice Dean Woo was not saying anything new. It was always the same: Robert "would have to bear the consequences" for his actions.

What would those consequences be? Would they be greater than he could bear?

After the assembly, students flocked to him, suggesting he compromise.

"You don't necessarily have to give up your faith," they said. "The school can't force you to do that. You can believe Sabbath in your heart while you sit in class on Saturday. The constitution protects the people's right to religious freedom, but you can't violate school regulations. Obey school rules and keep your faith in your heart. Attend class on Saturday, or you'll suffer for missing that day."

Should he do just that? Compromise? Should he keep Sabbath in his heart while sitting in a high-school classroom listening to a teacher's lecture?

The question was sure to arise every Monday in assembly. Robert wondered to himself, *Is it worth filling in requests to be excused from school to attend church on Sabbath, when I know they will be denied?* Trying to answer his own question, he reasoned, *Wouldn't it be easier to compromise? On Sabbath afternoon, after school, I could have private devotions in the park.* He dismissed the thought, but it continued to nag him. For the next few weeks, Robert resisted the urge.

As graduation neared, though, Robert feared he would be denied his diploma unless he reformed his attendance record. That punishment was indeed more than he could bear. Worse still, he might be expelled. If he were dismissed, no other school would accept him. Vice Dean Woo had been right about his future. If he continued to be a Sabbath keeper, the government would keep him waiting for a job indefinitely. Then, too, there was the *wai kiu* factor. His oldest brother,

John, now lived in California, and his father had been born in America. John was the only member of the family who had opted to take passage to America in 1950 just before his American passport expired. No one else in the family had up-to-date American passports. To make matters worse, his older sister, Darlene, was often sick with tuberculosis; her illness took her in and out of hospital. With John on the other side of the Pacific and Darlene ill, he bore the responsibilities of the oldest child. After his father had died of tuberculosis in June, 1950, his mother lost his father's income. Being a housewife, she lived off the income she earned by renting the lower two stories of her house. Though the rent was high, it was not enough; so if Robert couldn't land a job in the community, he could not support his aging mother. She needed him.[1] When news arrived that some Adventist students had been expelled, Robert struggled with his thoughts. Should he conform to the dean's wishes and attend school on Sabbath?

One Sabbath he awoke early, dressed in his uniform—a white shirt and long black trousers—and walked to school. With each step he hoped compromise would relieve the pressure. Soon he could see the school looming ahead. He proceeded past the courtyard, where some students were playing basketball. Entering the building, he marched down the hall, feeling almost certain he would attend class. It was the only way to stop hearing his name mentioned in Monday assemblies.

An immense conflict raged within him. On one hand, he wanted to worship in church; on the other hand, he didn't want to break school rules. Seeing the stairs that led to the roof, he climbed them. No one noticed. Up on the flat roof, undetected by anyone on the school grounds, Robert knelt and poured out his heart to God. He begged Jesus to give him the strength to do His will. It seemed as though he could hear Satan tempting him to yield. Then the words of a Chinese hymn came to mind: "Even though everyone forsakes You, by Your grace I will still be the loyal one!" Immediately, he faced his tormentor and sang him that song. The sacred lyrics scared the devil away!

On the roof that morning, Robert surrendered his life to Christ anew. Jesus restored his faith, and Robert put it into action. He decided to follow the example of the apostles and obey God rather than man. No longer fearing the consequences, he arose from his knees, marched down the steps, along the hall, past the ball field, and onto the street to church. No one in the school ever knew how close he'd come to attending class that Sabbath. When he sat in church that day, he was grateful that Jesus had helped him to do the right thing. He determined always to do all in his power, by God's grace, to be true to Jesus. He never again considered attending classes on Sabbath.

When the school year rolled to an end, the final exam fell on a Sabbath. Robert didn't attend. The school offered him a second chance, but the make-up test was scheduled on another Sabbath, so he skipped that one too. He wasn't allowed to graduate. Fortunately, the high school encouraged all of its students to enroll in college and pulled strings to help them enter. It had a perfect record and it was not about to have it spoiled. This enabled Robert to be accepted into college without graduating from high school.

Robert thought that the school had treated him well for one or more of three reasons, two of them earthly. First, he was a good student and, second, he was a *wai kiu* with family members in the United States. However, he could not discount the thought that God had blessed him for faithfully observing the Sabbath!

---

[1] This statement includes cultural assumptions. Chinese children are expected to support their parents no matter how much money the parents are making. Robert's mother was a housewife, but she was also a landlord. She owned a three-story house and rented out the first two floors to the railway ticket bureau. The rent was high because the house was huge. But Robert was obligated to supplement his mother's rent money.

CHAPTER 3

Marx Meets
the Messiah

In 1956, Robert watched with interest as a new movement emerged around him. Communist Party chairman Mao Zedong himself initiated the movement, which was called Let a Hundred Flowers Bloom. Before the movement, Chinese were forced to keep their opinions to themselves. While the "hundred flowers bloomed," however, the people were given an opportunity to speak freely about problems in the country. Most people welcomed the policy because they believed Chairman Mao had their best interests at heart. They thought the Party wanted to improve.

Tragically, they would discover that they had misunderstood the government's true intent. The movement was a plot to uncover enemies of the party, and it worked altogether too well. Many who stepped forward to criticize the government or to suggest improvements soon found themselves behind bars, while others had family members who were forced to pay for an executioner's bullet.

God used Mao's plot to His own advantage. When the government "let a hundred flowers bloom," it became the best time for church work in Shanghai. Restrictions against religion were removed, allowing evangelists to work freely. Adventism grew rapidly—flowering faster than any other denomination in China. The Communist leaders actually encouraged church activism and, not surprisingly, many youth joined the church, and a number entered the ministry. Among these were three Seventh-day Adventist youth who were appointed to attend the interdenominational seminary in Nanjing. Robert Huang was one of them.

Among Adventist church members these appointments were very controversial. Many of the older folk in the church wagged their heads, predicting that if the youth went to the seminary, it would be the end of their Christian experience because the interdenominational seminary was operated under the umbrella of the Communist government. Some folk thought the government intended to deliberately divide the church then conquer it. These concerned church members had reason to fear. Government leaders had stated that those who wished to conduct church work had to study at the seminary in Nanjing; therefore, it was strongly implied that those who did not attend could not be active. Because the school was run by the government, Marxism would be mingled with Christianity. How could anything good come out of a mix of atheism and monotheism? Certainly, the students would not be trained in the unique theology of the Advent movement. At best, these church members thought, if the three youths retained Christian theology, they would come out of the seminary thinking the same as members of any other Christian denominations[1] in Shanghai. In other words, they would be (as prophecy had predicted about the last days) false teachers—wolves cloaked in sheep's wool. The government, it turned out, was confident that Marxist dogma would destroy the seminarians and ultimately terminate church activism.

Others in the church were not worried about the government's agenda. They were happy that Robert had been selected. They compared him to Daniel and considered the other two as Daniel's friends. They hoped that these three would stand firm and, like Shadrach, Meshach, and Abednego, show the "Babylonians" in the seminary that Adventism was not a cult. They wanted the youth to prove to Christians that Adventists actually believed in Jesus Christ and were therefore Christian like them.

Robert went to Nanjing fully determined to be a Daniel. During the year he was at the seminary, he had no problem keeping Sabbath. He carefully selected his classes, and at the end of the year, the

Seventh-day Adventist Church in Shanghai ordained him to be a youth pastor.

In 1958, the government initiated the Great Leap Forward, which marked the end of the political, economic, intellectual, and religious freedoms that had bloomed with the Hundred Flowers. In practical terms, the government changed because it was desperate for resources and manpower. It called for workers to unite. It combined congregations of all denominations, including Seventh-day Adventists, until only ten percent of them were in operation, which effectively put ninety percent of the pastors out of work and left their church buildings available to be used as factories.

In compliance with the government, church leaders reduced services, and soon meetings were held only once a week. The government organized the Three-Self Church[2] and allowed priests and pastors from the Catholic, Christian,[3] and Adventist churches to serve in the church. All services were conducted on Sunday. Adventist ministers, though not allowed to preach on Sabbath, were granted the pulpit on Sunday. Some Adventist pastors held separate services outside the walls of the Three-Self Church. Other Adventist pastors and administrators gladly took the pulpit on Sunday and encouraged their members to attend. These preachers were grateful that the government allowed them to perform any religious activity—even on Sunday!

Some church leaders became the running dogs of the Communists; like dogs chasing sticks thrown by their masters, they mindlessly fulfilled the party's wishes and followed their every whim. Many found themselves parroting the Communist Party line, even though it countered what they knew to be true. They seemed not to care that theological error had been mingled with Adventist thought. Robert wondered how atheistic dogma could merge with Christian belief and remain faithful. Truly, Communism had a social gospel to boast of, but when it came to God's law, Robert felt a line had to be drawn.

After a time, the Three-Self Church told pastors that if they wanted to continue in active ministry, they must attend political meetings. Wishing to show their willingness to cooperate with the government, Adventist ministers and administrators informed the organizers that they would be willing to attend, provided the meetings were not held on the Sabbath. They were promised that it would not be a problem. With that assurance, the Adventist ministers joined. But no sooner were the classes organized than the pastors and church administrators were told that they must attend classes on Saturday. The Adventists felt confused, but trusting the earlier agreement, they did not show up. For the first session, the government was lenient.

During the second session, however, those who had failed to attend were punished. On Monday, many were ordered to write self-criticisms. This went on week after week, which became bothersome. Gradually, some Adventist ministers began to rationalize. For Robert, attending political meetings on Sabbath—even if it was with fellow clergy and administrators of his own church—was out of the question. He could not discuss Marxist, Leninist, and Maoist thought on the day God had set aside for Himself. Sabbath was a sacred time for heavenly thoughts.

Even though he knew the consequences, Robert did not show up for the political meetings on Sabbath. For those who did not attend on Sabbath, "struggle sessions" were set up every Monday to help monitor behavior. In them, members of the sessions struggled with individuals who resisted conformity. The meetings were designed to intimidate with increasing intensity. Robert became the center of unwanted attention. Initially, those in the meeting would stare at anyone who made no comment. The quiet one was expected to criticize himself or to report on someone else present at the meeting. If the look did not get the desired response, others in the group would point out the targeted individual's faults, pressuring him to confess. In a culture where all are expected to follow the norm, the nail that sticks up gets hit; therefore, someone who disagrees with the crowd gets hammered from all sides. Often the hammering becomes violent, and individuals are injured. With God's help, Robert endured the stares, criticism, and beatings and stood his ground.

On weekdays, church leaders, including members of the Adventist church, visited reluctant ministers to encourage them to fall in line. Soon only a small number of Adventist ministers refrained from attending the political meetings on Sabbath. Among them was Robert.

One day, he heard a knock on his door. When he answered the door, a couple of Adventist leaders were standing outside. He welcomed them in and served them herbal tea.

As they sipped from their teacups, one of the visitors, Yuen Fung, a handsome middle-aged woman, stated, "We miss you at the political meetings."

Robert replied, "I cannot attend political meetings on Sabbath."

Mrs. Yuen placed her cup in its saucer and asked, "Why so strict, Robert?"

"Six days we have to talk about earthly things, but the Sabbath—"

"We know all that." The woman's eyes glared. "We were church members before you were born." Her tone, once dismissive, waxed earnest. "Robert, now is a time to be flexible. If you're too rigid, you'll break. Can't you bend just a little?"

"The tree that doesn't resist the wind is crooked," Robert replied firmly. "How can we be Seventh-day Adventists if we don't keep the Sabbath holy?"

Yuen Fung smiled and leaned forward in her seat. "If we work with the Party, we can do more for the Lord. Please listen to Auntie Fung's[4] humble suggestion, Robert. Why not conduct sundown worship early, close the Sabbath, and then attend the meetings? That's what we do!"

Attempting to appeal to their conscience, Robert spoke frankly, saying, "Thank you for your advice, but I cannot compromise my principles. Closing Sabbath early won't make it sundown. I must guard the edges of the Sabbath."

The other visitor grew impatient. "Robert, the government has asked you to attend these political meetings. You forget that Scripture tells us to obey the government."

Quoting scripture, Robert replied, "The Bible also tells us that we are not to obey the government if man's laws conflict with God's laws. The Sabbath is one of God's laws."

The church leaders became angry. "China is only a socialist state. It has not reached Communism yet, as Russia has. Russia has a five-day work week. You must work Sabbaths until Communism comes to China. Then you can have Sabbath off."

"I'm not sure that China will reach the Communist phase within my lifetime. Why should I wait for something, when I don't know when it will happen?" Robert's remark so enraged the church leaders that they stormed out of his house immediately. Their parting words were, "Think deeply about what we have talked about. The struggle sessions can only get worse. You have to bear the consequences for your own decisions." Robert bade them farewell politely and shut the door behind them, knowing he was not only a marked man but also a "watched" man.

It would be only a matter of time before he would meet the agent assigned to tail him.

---

[1] The English-speaking world in China divides Christianity into three groups: Catholic, Christian, and Adventist. Protestant denominations in China do not call themselves Protestant. Instead they call themselves Christian, strongly implying that neither Catholics nor Adventists are Christian.

[2] The Chinese Marxists considered Christianity to be a Western implant into Chinese society. They believed that forcing it to be self-organized, self-supporting, and self-propagating would cause it to die a natural death because only foreign missionaries and Western aid kept the fledgling religion alive. For good measure, the government seminary trained the ministers in Marxist ideology, thinking its superior logic would replace Christian thought. The government didn't trust Christians after they had helped the Marxists overthrow the Kuomintang regime. To help maintain its control, the government forced ecumenism upon all the churches, requiring Catholics, Christians (Protestants), and Adventists to unite under one roof every Sunday. Many pastors joined; others went underground, which, ironically, made controlling the situation more difficult for China. Sadly, this would lead to great persecution.

[3] Protestant

[4] In Asia older women refer to themselves as aunties—proverbial aunties with no family connection. Children call any adult friend of their parents "uncle" or "auntie."

CHAPTER 4

Working Underground

Not long after the Adventist leaders had tried to convince Robert Huang to toe the Communist Party line, he was called before the Three-Self Church in Shanghai. He knew his refusal to attend political classes offered every Saturday had gotten him into trouble. It was difficult for him to believe that even the Adventist leaders had encouraged him to break the Sabbath. And now the Three-Self Church was making an example of him.

When he entered the church, the Three-Self leaders came over to him and forced him to stand before the podium. Many prominent people from all denominations sat in the pews and began criticizing him. "Bow your head!" they commanded. "Repent!"

Robert stood before them and smiled.

"Rein in your stubborn horse!" they shouted. Robert noted that some of the pastors and church members who were shouting at him were Adventists. "Join the socialist way!" They yelled louder than the others.

Remembering what the Bible said about pearls and swine, he remained silent. All around him, the church was in turmoil, yet his heart was at peace.

Eventually, Lin Fong, the leader of the Three-Self Church in Shanghai, said, "It appears that even if Robert Huang bowed outwardly, he won't bow inwardly." Mr. Lin told one side of the church to be quiet.

The members on that side obeyed. Soon the whole church was silent. Eagerly everyone watched for the leader's next move.

Lin Fong turned to Robert and said, "You may go now. If the church can't help you, perhaps the government will." It was a strong hint. Robert might be arrested.

Robert left the Three-Self church, but he didn't go home. Instead, he visited a couple of elderly ladies, both Adventist church members, and told them about his experience. "My situation is grave," he concluded. "Can I ask a favor? If anything happens to me, will you call my family and inform them?" The elderly women kindly agreed. With that, Robert returned to attending his political classes on the weekdays and skipping them on Sabbath. Nobody said anything to him. Everything seemed normal—almost. There was, however, the ever-present specter of being arrested.

Some time later Robert learned that many who had criticized him in the Three-Self Church had been impressed. They marveled that he had stood firm for his beliefs even though all the others had been confused. It seemed to them that Robert had something they lacked. Several members from other denominations became interested in what Adventists had to teach. On hearing the news, Robert rejoiced that the inner peace he had felt that day had somehow shone through, and he thanked God for giving him, like the apostle Paul before, a unique opportunity to witness.

Soon another session of political meetings was formed for church members. Robert Huang's mother and elder sister were asked to attend, but Robert himself was not. He suspected that it was for two reasons. First, if he were absent, others might conclude that he had been arrested. Second, he felt sure that government officials and church leaders didn't want his attitude in the meetings. Likely they feared it would be contagious.

****

After 1958, Robert joined one of the Adventist underground churches. Its members refused to join the Three-Self movement. These members met in parks or in church members' homes. As with the early church in the days of pagan Rome, everything was conducted in secret. Not secretly enough, however. That year, 1958, many Adventist leaders active in the underground church were imprisoned, including Vast Ocean Chu. The first leader arrested was Glorious Country Gong. He had aroused the authorities' anger because he loved to talk about his friend Jesus with anyone he met. Sentenced to twenty years hard labor at a camp in Tsinghai, his fate was supposed to reflect that of all Christians throughout China. No one expected him to return alive.[1] With so many arrested in such a short time, Robert feared his turn was coming soon.

One Sabbath Robert set out for a nearby park. Proceeding down the street, he passed through a busy shopping district. Crowds were examining the goods in the stores. Robert entered one of the shops and looked into a display case containing stoneware tea sets. When he thought he had looked at them for a sufficient period, he quickly looked around at every corner of the store, examining the faces of the people shopping. No one looked suspicious. Moving to another counter, he repeated the process. Convinced that he was not being followed, he left the store and walked to the park.

Seeing a secluded bench, he sat down and waited, watching for both suspicious and familiar faces. Eventually, some Adventists arrived. Their number was desirably small. The larger the group, the more suspicious it would look. As the recent arrests attested, attracting attention was unwise. Robert spoke a few words of encouragement to them. They discussed a Bible text, and then, one by one, the people dispersed until he alone remained on the bench. When he thought the time was right, he, too, left.

Not far from the park was a church member's home. Answering his knock, the member welcomed him in. They talked awhile of spiritual things. Occasionally, their discussion was interrupted by a knocking. Soon a small group sat around the living room, singing favorite hymns and listening to Robert's teaching from the Bible. After a while, they shared communion and washed each other's feet. As irregularly as they had arrived, members left stealthily, hoping not to be noticed by government authorities, and new ones arrived. They, too, wanted to hear what Robert had to say about Jesus. The gospel was shared, as was the bread and the grape juice. When all had gone, Robert arose and walked to a nearby hospital to visit patients. As the sun set on the Sabbath, he returned home. It had been a long day, but he felt refreshed.

The next week, Robert set out for a church member's home on Sabbath. En route, he tried to lose himself in crowded streets or followed less-traveled roads. Arriving at an apartment, he knocked. The door opened, and he slipped inside. Just as he and his friends had settled comfortably, they heard another knock. The apartment's owner answered the door.

Outside stood a police officer in uniform. "Who came to visit you?"

When Robert showed his face, the policeman pushed his way in. "*Ni nar!*" he demanded gruffly. "Who are you?"

"Robert Huang." He smiled at the police officer.

Without returning the smile, the policeman barked, "Give me your red card." A red card was a red plastic folder that bore an individual's identity. On it was a photo of the bearer sealed with a government chop[2] and the owner's name, address, and work unit. People in China were divided into work units, which were more like units in the community. Each commune had a leader who was responsible for the people living in it. Usually the members in the commune all worked in the same factory. Occasionally there were members who were waiting for work or who had refused the work the government had offered them. Robert was in this category. He received a meager stipend from the government until work could be found. Life would have been absolutely miserable for his family if he were not *wai kiu*. His American relatives supplemented his income.

Reaching into his pocket, Robert pulled out his red card, and the officer snatched it away, opened it, read it, and returned it. Without a word, the police officer turned and left.

Robert concluded the obvious. He was being watched. Now the authorities knew his name, address, and occupation—unemployed pastor. In the People's working paradise, where no one is unemployed, the government would say that he was a pastor awaiting his assignment from the party. Perhaps they would check his dossier and realize he was a pastor who had refused to join the Three-Self Church. From this point on, Robert would need to double his precautions. Soon the government would have evidence that he was working for the underground church. Only trouble could follow that discovery.

Undeterred, Robert sat back down in his host's living room and completed the worship service before he left.

****

Walking down the street on another Sabbath morning, Robert heard someone hail him. "Where are you going?" he asked.

Instantly, Robert concluded that the man was a plain-clothes agent. Like Abram when he lied to Pharaoh, Robert's faith in God momentarily faltered. "I might go shopping," he said, fudging out of fear. The answer was only partly false. He was going to the market, but not to shop because it was the Sabbath. The road to the underground church was not straight. He often turned into the open market and mingled with the customers, just to confuse spies like this agent.

The plain-clothes agent looked at Robert knowingly. "Probably you will go to Miss Yang's house."

Shock tingled up and down Robert's spine. That was exactly where he was headed. Seeing the agent grin cleverly, Robert guessed that his surprise had shown on his face.

The government was clearly zeroing in on him.

Some time later, a government agent in uniform visited him at his home. Coming straight to the point, he stated, "You're a *wai kiu*, Robert Huang. We know that your brother emigrated to the United States back in 1950. It was before his American passport expired on August 5, 1950. Your American-born father helped your brother migrate to America through Hong Kong. Would you like a visa to join him in America?"

Thoughts raced through Robert's head. Travel visas were not granted easily in China. Getting a visa to America was almost impossible. Only those favored by Party authorities could obtain one. Why was he being offered one? What had he, a pastor of an illegal church organization, done to gain the favor of an atheistic government bent upon destroying superstition within its realm? How should he answer? Tempted to accept, Robert considered the consequences. If they granted him a visa, he could leave the pressures of Liberated China and never fear arrest again. But what would happen to his work in Shanghai? Who could continue it? Most of the Adventist pastors were members of the Three-Self Church. If they were not, they were imprisoned and doing hard labor. He felt as though he were Elijah—the only righteous man in Israel capable of leading.

Suddenly, it occurred to him. No visa had been offered him. The agent had merely asked if he wanted one. Surely it was a trap! If he showed interest, it might "prove" he was disloyal to the motherland. Perhaps, Robert reasoned, if he requested one, the government officer would accuse him of espionage and arrest him immediately. Then the poor church members would become sheep without a shepherd. Obviously, Robert thought, the government aimed to stop his work. Apparently he had not been locked up before now because of his *wai kiu* status. Was the government changing its tactics? Did they now hope to use the fact he was an overseas Chinese against him? Choosing his words carefully, Robert replied, "Thank you for your kind offer, sir, but I won't need a visa to America. I'm Chinese, and Shanghai is my home. My family needs me here."

Watching the agent's manner as he made a hasty retreat confirmed Robert's suspicions.

****

Arriving in a park one Sabbath in 1962, Robert found, to his surprise, a crowd of thirty church members awaiting him. This was more than he had expected. Generally, the members arrived more discretely. Groups this size could only arouse suspicion.

As dangerous as it was both for himself and for them, there was nothing he could do. How could he send them away? Sitting down on a bench, he fed them spiritual food, dismissed them, and hoped for the best. When he heard no unwanted knocks on his door for six days, he dared conclude the authorities had not noticed. Perhaps he was no longer watched.

Then, on the morning of the seventh day—the following Sabbath—Robert was awakened by an attendant in his apartment complex. "You have a phone call," she said. In the 1960s, few Shanghainese had telephones in their homes. They were lucky to have one public phone station on the main floor of their apartment building. All calls were processed through an operator. Grabbing some clothes, Robert dressed and dashed downstairs to the front desk. On his way he saw a plain-clothes agent standing at the entrance. Immediately, Robert recognized him as the same agent who, four years earlier, had hailed him on the street and predicted, with stunning accuracy, precisely where Robert was going.

"You have a phone call from Miss Liu," he said.

Robert smiled to himself. So Miss Liu was on the phone. Judging from the past, the agent was probably correct. How did he know so much about Robert?

The policeman added, "She asked *me* to tell you that she was calling."

The statement seemed quite odd. If he had heard him correctly, the agent had said, "She asked me"—him, a plain-clothes government agent—"to tell you"—Robert, an underground pastor—"that she"—one of Robert's church members—"was calling"—on the telephone. *She* asked a plain-clothes agent to pass a message to him. Why would she tell a government agent she was calling—unless she had betrayed him! Robert grew suspicious. "If *she* called me on the phone, why did she tell *you* to tell me she was on the line?"

The agent flashed a clever grin, similar to the one Robert had seen before. "Come with me."

Instantly, Robert knew that no one had called. The plain-clothes agent had only wanted to see his reaction. Luckily, he thought to himself as he followed the government agent, he had seen through the trick and given nothing away. Ahead in the distance, he saw the walls of the police station.

---

[1] Happily, his Friend Jesus remembered him. After surviving more than twenty years in Tsinghai's hard labor camp, Glorious Country Gong would become known as "the man who couldn't be killed." You can read the full story of this remarkable man in *The Man Who Couldn't Be Killed* (Nampa, Idaho: Pacific Press, 1995).

[2] A chop is an object, sometimes made of stone, with a name carved in bas relief on the bottom. As used by the ancient kings of Persia, it is stamped into a seal to show authority.

CHAPTER 5

Detention!

Inside the police station, officers escorted Robert down a long hallway with a polished wooden floor and into a room with a large wooden desk and sat him down to interrogate him. "Where were you last Saturday?" they demanded repeatedly.

"I went to the park."

"What did you do in the park? Whom did you meet?"

Attempting to learn what they knew about him without disclosing anything, a common practice among Chinese, Robert feigned ignorance and volunteered nothing. By listening carefully to their questions, he ascertained both what the police knew and did not know about his activities. Soon the questions became monotonously repetitive. Robert stopped listening.

Seeing that they were getting nowhere, one of the agents produced a folder, pulled out some photographs, and laid them on the table for Robert to see. They showed him preaching in the park the previous week. Taken from various angles, the faces of the thirty church members were quite clear.

"You must take full responsibility for their arrests!" an agent declared. "Your antiParty activities must cease. Encourage Christians to register at the Three-Self Church and your benevolent government will be merciful. Rein in your stubborn horse! Continue teaching superstition and, as you can see, you'll endanger others."

"Where are these people now?" Robert asked.

An officer laughed. "Some are serving three-year sentences in a hard labor camp."

Stunned by the news, Robert longed to visit with them and comfort them. An agent's question brought his mind back to the interrogation room. "Do you have anything to tell us?"

When Robert said he didn't, the police officers ended the interview by saying, "We're going to give you a warning this time. Terminate your counterrevolutionary activities, or bear the consequences."

Agents transferred him to the front office but did not grant him permission to leave. Ignoring him completely, some of the agents stood idly behind a curved wooden table, while others chatted amongst themselves. Seeing some of the clerks wolfing down rice reminded Robert that it was lunchtime and that he had missed breakfast.

Soon dusk approached; Sabbath was almost over. Having missed all his appointments with church members, his work had been successfully thwarted. There was nothing he could do to turn back the time. What of his family? There had been no time to inform them of his detention. Were they worried? Robert approached an officer, "Please, sir, may I call my family?"

"No," the officer barked.

"I want to tell them where I am," Robert urged.

"It won't be necessary because they were informed by the police."

Robert became quiet.

An officer offered him some steamed bread. Starved though he was, Robert was afraid he might be charged for the meal. He didn't want to pay for a meal during the Sabbath hours. While scrupulous about following the command to observe the Sabbath, he overlooked the law prohibiting deception. Wanting badly to be reunited with his family, he said politely, "I don't want to eat." The bread was hastily removed. Thinking this officer friendly, Robert asked courteously, "May I go home now?"

"No!" the officer barked.

After the sun set, Robert asked to call his family again. Again the request was denied. With nothing better to do, Robert initiated a watching game. His rules were simple. He watched the police while they were watching him.

Eventually, an officer approached. "You're released now, but let today be a lesson for you! Obey the law! We'll be watching you."

Robert respectfully thanked him for his instruction, excused himself, stepped out into the darkness, and hurried through the busy streets toward home. Stepping up to the entryway of the railway ticketing agency that rented the two lower floors of his mother's house, Robert opened the door. He then ran up the three flights of stairs to his mother's apartment and knocked on the door. Once inside the living room, his family urged him to sit on the big wooden chair that doubled as a bed. With a great show of reluctance, Robert, after being coaxed repeatedly, eventually agreed to sit on it. Once he had sat down, the family gathered around him, eager to hear his news. That night, it was difficult to tell who, if anyone, was the happier—he to see his family, or they to see him. After they had settled down and served tea, Robert said, "I tried to call but couldn't. Were you notified?"

"We know nothing," his mother replied.

So, Robert thought to himself, the police had had no intention of following through on their promise to inform his family.

"What happened?" his sister asked.

"The Lord is good. I was detained, questioned, and released." Robert did not wish to involve his family needlessly. Knowing that he was a watched man, deep down he asked himself how much more time would be allowed him before he could no longer shepherd his flock in Shanghai.

CHAPTER 6

Don't Wait for Me

One barren winter day in January, 1964, a couple of years after his day in detention, Robert was going about his routine underground ministry when he chanced to meet the brother of a friend a—young woman named Mary.

"Mary's back in town!" her brother exclaimed. "She's back from the frontier and home with me!"

The news set Robert's heart racing. He hadn't seen Mary in five years. He felt sure he could never forget the first time he had seen her, nine years earlier, in 1955. They were seminarians who happened to be attending the same church one Sabbath. Her dress was simple, and her hair covered her neck, which was out of style at the time. Smiling to himself, he couldn't help wondering if she had cut it herself. It lacked the professional touch common to trendy Shanghainese. He recalled seeing two fashion-minded girls turn around in their pew with a curious stare at Mary's hair because it was so long. Robert had wanted to scold them for their rudeness but noticed that Mary didn't bat an eye. This made a deep impression on him.

Not long afterward, Robert and Mary had both joined a class in acupuncture. As underground church workers they had thought that, like the apostle Paul who made tents for a living, they needed an employable skill. While taking the class, they had grown acquainted.

Don't Wait for Me

Would those seeds of affection grow and yield fruit? He hoped they would. But with a potential prison term on his horizon, Robert had decided to leave the watering to God.

As he walked home he wondered to himself, *Does she still have that lovely fair skin and the same gorgeous round face? Would her eyes have the same sparkle when she looks at me?* The two had grown close before they had become separated by thousands of kilometers when Mary had gone to work in the western province of Xingjiang. Happily, her brother had not joined the Xingjiang Movement that had taken Mary to the frontier.

A few days later, Robert decided to visit Mary. As he stood by the trolley stop, his mind wandered. It had been so many years since they had last seen each other. Could he get a date with Mary? How did she feel about him? What would it be like when they met after so long?

The clang of a trolley bell awoke him from his reverie. Hopping onto the crowded vehicle, he stood as it meandered through the streets heading ever closer to Mary. Closing his eyes, he remembered the last time he had seen her. The picture remained with him as though it were only days before. He saw himself standing on the platform at the train station, bidding her farewell. How could he forget that time?

That year of 1959, Robert recalled, the year after he had lost his job as a Seventh-day Adventist pastor for refusing to attend political meetings on Sabbath, was the year Mary's school in Nanjing was shut down and she found herself without work. While she was away at school, her father had been arrested as a counterrevolutionary for translating the religious writings of Ellen G. White. He received a twelve-year sentence.

Depressed, Mary had assumed her job prospects were slim. After all, she had three black marks in her dossier. She was an underground Christian, a seminary-educated "intellectual," and the daughter of a convicted counterrevolutionary.

Under the circumstances, she had welcomed an opportunity provided for doctors, nurses, teachers, and other intellectuals to move to Xingjiang, the western-most province in China. By going, she had hoped to show her patriotism to the government and erase some, if not all, of those strikes against her. None of those who agreed to go were aware of what they would encounter. Along with its harsh ter-

51

rain, Xingjiang boasted nomadic tribes that herded livestock much as Moses and David had in ancient times. Mary had been assigned to work in the post office.

Robert, still unemployed and still watched by Chairman Mao's secret agents, had remained in Shanghai. With the help of payment from the government doled out to those who were waiting for work, along with some support from his brother in California, he had been able to serve as an underground pastor to a troubled congregation.

On the memorable day that Mary left, he had watched the train shrink into a dot on the horizon. Their lives had taken divergent paths. Would they cross again? Neither one had ever told the other, "I love you." *Will we get back together?* he had wondered. It seemed impossible then. Yet she had returned. Had five years in Xingjiang changed her?

As his trolley turned a corner, Robert saw his stop and shouted, "*Sha cher!*" loudly enough for the driver to know he needed to get off and then began squeezing between the passengers until he reached the exit. The trolley slowed to a halt, and Robert jumped down to the sidewalk. Walking up the street, he soon arrived at Mary's brother's home. When she appeared at the door, he noticed she had lost some weight and that her hair was shorter. She looked lovelier than he could imagine.

They left the house to stroll in a park and talk. To break the ice, she took a box of raisins out of her purse, opened the box, and shared some. Robert politely tasted a few. "Do you like raisins?" she asked. "I brought them from Xingjiang. They're native to the province."

Soon it became apparent that even though they had lived at opposite ends of China and in environments as different as night and day, the spirit between them remained the same. As they wandered through the park, she told him about the visit she and her brother had made to their father in prison. It was the first thing she had done upon her return to Shanghai.

Talk though they did, they didn't say much. Robert didn't know what to say. Had it been too long? Was it still too soon to declare their affections? He thought to himself, *I'm a pastor who has no trouble talking in front of a group of people, but in private conversations with anyone—especially an attractive young woman—I'm shy.* What was there to say?

His future seemed so uncertain. Rumors were rife. Certain that he had been branded antisocialist, he thought he would be arrested soon. Instead of saying to Mary that it would be only a matter of time before he was arrested for doing illegal church work, he said, "Mary, many Adventist pastors are now serving prison terms." Would she know what he meant? It was dangerous for her to be associated with him, especially if he were arrested. Because her father was a counterrevolutionary, if it became known that she was his girlfriend, her life could only get worse.

It seemed that she did understand. But try as he might to discourage her, Robert found that his dim prospects did not disturb her.

All too soon the walk ended, and Robert rode the trolley back to his home.

Not long afterward, Mary moved out of her brother's house to live with her aunt.

****

Answering a knock on his door on Sabbath morning, September 26, 1964, Robert saw the same plain-clothes agent who, he recalled, had detained him at the police station for one day. That particular Sabbath Robert had gotten off with just a warning, but his church members had not fared so well. Some of the thirty to whom he had preached had been sentenced to serve three years in a hard-labor camp.

The agent burst inside and looked around, hoping to find Robert conducting an underground church service or perhaps see evidence of clandestine activities. He found no one in the house other than Robert's immediate family. Dejected, the agent sat down and said scathingly, "We have received many reports about you and your covert activities from all over the country."

"What do you mean?" Robert exclaimed, feigning ignorance to cover his fear.

"We have already carried out the Socialist Education Movement, but you stubbornly persist in preaching and defying us. Now hand over your letters!"

"What letters?" Robert asked.

"All the letters from your church members. We know you have them in your possession."

Robert knew exactly what letters he meant and where they were. He had written and received many letters over the past two years. Painfully aware that he was under surveillance, he had gone further underground since his brief detention in 1962. Rather than meeting with his congregation at the park, he had ministered to them through handwritten letters, articles, and poems. Soon replies were pouring in until he had a large bag of letters from church members, all of them personally answered. In some of the letters he had written epistles reminiscent of Paul and the apostles; in others, devotional poetry and hymns. Despite the risk to himself, he wrote because he thought each time the letters were reread, the members would be blessed anew. He hoped the words would bolster their faith, strengthening them in the hard times they were experiencing. As he thought about the letters, he knew that he had to protect the members who had trusted him by writing them. Mustering his courage, he replied, "I refuse to surrender them. Not a word in them is against the government."

"That's for us to determine!"

Apparently, the officer had reason to believe Robert had plotted to overthrow the government, which could not have been further from the truth. For the past two years, when he wasn't writing encouraging letters, his underground activities had included conducting private devotions at Adventists' homes on Sabbath, visiting the sick in hospitals, and preaching at funerals. Notably, on one occasion, he had presided over the funeral service for Vast Ocean Chu's father, who, sadly, had passed away while his son was still a prisoner. Vast Ocean had been forced to "learn from the peasants" while working on the harsh farms in Anwi Province, infamous for its poor crop yields. It was an especially difficult task for a man trained in scholarly pursuits. Chu's father had served in diplomatic posts, so his funeral had been packed with low-ranking cadres and local Communist leaders. No one else would conduct the service because of Chu's father's fame, and Vast Ocean himself, a minister and church administrator, was a convicted counterrevolutionary. Seeing it as a God-given opportunity to witness to government officials, Robert had preached fearlessly. Later he would question whether his daring had actually been mere foolishness, for words he had told the officials would return to haunt him.

In the interim, having had no brush with the authorities for almost two years, Robert began to think his underground activities had gone undetected. While arguably safer than organizing illegal public meetings in the park, letter writing entailed a greater risk—tangible evidence of "covert" activity.

Deciding it was rude not to speak to the agent, he asked, "Do you have any evidence against me?"

The officer, speechless, angrily thumped his fist against the table, knocking over a glass of water. Standing up, he rushed into Robert's bedroom and then into his study.

Scared though Robert was, he hid his fears. Trying to fish information out of the agent, he stated, "I get so many letters, how can I know the precise ones you have in mind?"

"Probably you know a Miss Lin. From time to time, I've seen you visit her at her home." A sly grin spread across the agent's face when he detected recognition in Robert's eye. "She informed us of your clandestine operation." Revealing his primary source, the agent continued to list the names of other church members who had written to him. "Seems Miss Lin said something about a bag full of letters. Does this mean anything to you?"

Robert wondered whether Miss Lin had been tortured before she had reported him. Or had she been seeking merit? Probably she knew little of China's new constitution.

Looking the officer in the eye, Robert asked, "Do you have a search warrant?"

Admitting he had none, the agent asked politely, "Will you let me come inside your room and look for the letters I need?"

Robert graciously but firmly refused.

The agent grinned. "If I recall correctly, your mother owns this house. May I speak with her?"

Robert urged his mother not to get involved, saying, "Mom, please go to the kitchen. This has nothing to do with you." Robert knew that, without a warrant, the agent couldn't search boxes and drawers.

The agent insisted, and she agreed to speak with him. Soon he was back in Robert's room. The bag of letters the agent sought was next to

Robert's desk, but providentially, the agent failed to see it. According to the law, all he could do was to pick up items at random, which he did. Spying a set of Ellen G. White's *Spirit of Prophecy* on the desk, he opened them, found a few letters inside, and confiscated both the letters and the books, then hastily exited. As he left, he turned and said, "I'll give you one last chance to reconsider. Don't miss it, or you will learn from personal experience what will happen to you."

Robert laughed inwardly but said nothing.

The agent continued, "It'd be better if you cooperated. Now you alone must bear the consequences for your blatant obstinacy. At least I'm not leaving empty-handed. These books and letters will bolster my case. Don't forget: Teaching religion in Liberated China is not allowed."

As he stepped outside, his parting words were, "Oh, pardon me. It seems that I failed to introduce myself. I'm Officer Cheung Kin. Expect me back—with a warrant!"

As soon as the agent was out of sight, Robert hastily sifted through the contents of the large bag and then burned the more sensitive letters. He hid others under the beds of his family members. Thinking back on the ones he had burned, those listed by the agent touched him most.

****

Two days later, Robert dashed to the public phone booth to call Mary. He urgently needed to speak with her. He must throw caution to the wind and see her one more time, before it might be forever too late. But he knew he couldn't be reckless. Eyes were upon him. Ears were listening to his conversations.

He noticed that the neighbor across the street was looking out the window. Was she spying on him again? She had reported him in the past.

When Mary came on the line, he arranged to meet her in half an hour. Hurrying to her house, he checked the area for familiar faces, friendly or not. Seeing none, he knocked.

Mary answered quickly. Together they walked the crowded boulevard near her home. The park was too dangerous. There was safety in numbers. To make certain he wasn't being followed, Robert slowed their pace and then quickened it. Seeing no one follow his lead, he dared hope no one was watching.

Mustering up his courage, he said, "Mary, my situation is critical. I'm making preparations in case I'm arrested."

"I'll pray for you. May God's will be done." Her encouraging words shot strength into Robert.

As he escorted her home, he wanted to tell her that he didn't expect her to wait for him, but he couldn't say it in so many words. Rather than speak directly, he employed the principles of the Chinese eight-legged essay, which allow a person to talk around a point and leave the interpretation to the receiver. "Mary," he said. "We have many brothers in the Lord. Many are better than I." As badly as he wanted to spend the rest of his life with her, deep down in his heart he wanted her to have only the best.

Mary made no reply, leaving Robert to wonder. Had she misunderstood him? Or by silence did she mean she was willing to wait? He dared not ask.

Again it seemed that the walk ended too quickly, and he headed for the trolley stop, feeling sad. He had some idea of what lay ahead for his life.

CHAPTER 7

Living on Borrowed Time

Standing on the trolley as it jostled along toward his home, Robert realized that China's Liberation Day was fast approaching. It always came nine days before Nationalist's Day, the tenth day of the tenth month, which marked the day when, in 1911, Imperial China became a republic. Since 1949, October 1 had been Liberation Day. Robert remembered that day in 1949 very well, when the Communists forced Nationalist president Chiang Kai-shek to flee across the Taiwan Strait to the island of Taiwan. Afterward, the first of October had become a huge holiday for the Chinese under Communist rule, exceeded only by Chinese New Year. It was also a time when local authorities swept the country clean of bad elements, such as counterrevolutionaries like him.

Certain that his arrest was imminent, Robert made preparations, before he returned home from his date with Mary, by visiting a church member who would get married during the Nationalist Holiday. After congratulating him and giving him a white linen sheet as a gift, Robert said, "I hope that one day we'll be dressed in white linen robes to attend the Lamb's marriage feast in heaven. I'm sorry I cannot be with you at your wedding. Perhaps you'll learn later why I can't take part in your feast. Thank you for inviting me. My heart and prayers will be with you." After the appropriate farewells, he departed.

Living on Borrowed Time

At about two in the afternoon, he returned home and ate hurriedly.

An hour and a half later, he and Elder Sister[1] ironed their holiday clothes then cleaned the dishes. As he washed his bowl and plate, he chatted with her about the plain-clothes agent who had come for his letters two days earlier.

Suddenly there was a loud banging on the door.

Looking down from his third-story window, Robert saw two police officers standing at the side door on the ground floor. One was in uniform, the other in plain clothes. With them was a woman. The plain-clothes agent was the very same one who had been hounding him for years. Robert thought, *To mention the wolf's name is to see the same!*

Turning to Elder Sister, he said quickly, "They're here!" She started to her feet. The sound of the officers clomping up the wooden stairs grew nearer. In a moment the three officers were knocking at the back door. Without waiting, they barged inside.

"Come sit in the living room," Robert said nonchalantly.

"I'm Officer Cheung Kin. Remember me?" the plain-clothed agent asked, smiling broadly. "I think the last time we met you asked for one of these." He extracted an arrest warrant from his pocket and ordered Robert to sign. After Robert had complied, Officer Cheung said, "Remove your watch!"

Robert obeyed.

Instantly, the agent placed Robert's arms behind his back, whipped out a set of handcuffs, and snapped them around Robert's wrists. Feeling the handcuffs slip into place, Robert praised God that his mother was out on a walk with a relative. Had she seen his arrest, it might have been more than she could endure.

Pushing Robert into his bedroom, the officers closed the curtain and began rushing about the house. Overturning tables and chairs and Robert's mattress, they tore the room apart as they searched for incriminating evidence.

Having his bedroom ransacked bothered Robert not at all. He began singing a favorite hymn, "How firm a foundation, ye saints of the Lord."

Irritated, Officer Cheung asked, "Young man, why do you sing?"

"I know I've committed no crime," Robert replied. "I've done nothing against China or against the Chinese. It's all about religion." After a pause, he gestured toward the female officer and added, "I'm trying to witness to that young lady over there."

Unimpressed, Officer Cheung snorted, "Go ahead—laugh now! You'll have plenty of time to laugh after you're behind bars."

Searching every drawer, they found nothing, though the officer in uniform did browse through a bag of books. His interest was aroused by a book containing many Arabic numerals. Seeing that it had raised questions in the officer's mind, Robert explained in a matter-of-fact tone, "It's a logarithmic table, not a code book."

A few minutes later the officer in uniform picked up a picture of Elder Brother that showed him dressed in his American naval uniform standing beside a boat. Suspiciously, he asked, "Who's he? What does he do?"

"He's Elder Brother. He lives in America," Robert replied. Obviously disappointed, the officer put the picture down and resumed his search.

At around five in the afternoon, one of the officers demanded, "Where are the letters?"

How could he reply? If he were to say something like, "Probably all of the letters have been destroyed," which was true, he would only feed fuel to their flame. They would retort, "That means there may be some left. Where are they?" He did not wish to hand them over. Trying to avoid getting others into trouble unnecessarily, Robert decided to remain silent.

Shoving him around, they gruffly pushed him from room to room throughout the house, as if they somehow expected him to produce the letters. All the while, they tried to prevent him from having contact with his mother, who had returned from her walk.

Robert was back in his room again. In a coverup attempt to spare his mother from the trauma of seeing her son arrested, Officer Cheung told her, "We wish to take him to join a new study group." Then out of feigned respect, they requested her permission.

With tears in her eyes, she came into Robert's room and said, "Go with these young men and study with them for a while." After she left, they shoved him out into the living room. Out of the corner of his eye he could see his sister and his mother. Elder Sister was packing some clothes, towels, and a blanket for him.

"Take more!" the officer in uniform stated knowingly. "The weather will be cold." Taking the hint, she added warm clothes. Robert thought that surely the winter of his life had begun.

Soon he was whisked through the kitchen and out of the living room. Mentally he said Good-bye to the coal burner in the small kitchen, the big wooden chair in the living room, and the darkly varnished tables from which they had eaten many a delicious meal. Glancing quickly around his simple, yet lovely home, where he had spent precious time with his family and fellow church members, he gazed lovingly at his mother and saw tears welling up in her eyes. "Mother, please don't cry." She nodded her gray locks and forced back the tears.

"Don't be worried," Robert assured his relatives. Turning to his sister, he added, "Tell Mary. Comfort her." Trusting in the words of the hymn, "All the Way My Savior Leads Me," he wasn't worried about himself or what might happen to him. Instead he was fearful about his family's future. His new outlaw status as a counterrevolutionary meant that, in the government's eyes, his family might be traitors. Feeling that this could be the last time he would ever see his family together, he wanted them to have good memories. In his time of trouble, he sought only his family's comfort and happiness.

A jolt from Officer Cheung brought Robert back from his thoughts. Tiring of their fruitless search, the officers shoved Robert downstairs. At the bottom of the first-floor staircase, the plain-clothes agent placed an overcoat around Robert's shoulders so that no one outside would see Robert in handcuffs. Then he thrust Robert out the front door and onto the street, where a black 1940 sedan awaited him. Pushed into the middle of the back seat, he found himself flanked by officers.

Appraising his situation, relief flooded his nerves. If, as the sedan rode through the streets, anyone saw him inside, they would not suspect he was under arrest. Instead, they might think him honored. Very few people in Shanghai even hailed a taxi in those days unless they were about to attend a wedding or funeral. Having traveled only by bus or trolley for the past fifteen years, Robert had never even ridden in a car. Being escorted by two guards in the back of a black sedan was a rare privilege indeed.

Hopping into the front seat, the driver slipped the key into its slot, revved up the engine, and paraded the sedan down narrow streets. Robert stared out the window. He couldn't help asking himself, *Where am I going?*

[1] In Chinese culture it is not respectful for a younger sibling to address an older sibling by the given name; instead older siblings are called Elder Sister or Elder Brother or Second Sister (if the younger sibling has more than one older sister).

CHAPTER 8

Mind Games

The sedan passed through three pairs of high iron gates, each of which was opened by smiling guards and promptly closed and locked after the sedan drove through. After passing through the third iron gate, Robert found himself at a prison complex. Next to the main door he read in Chinese characters, "Number One Detention Block." At last he knew where he was going.

Before the sedan came to a complete stop, the prison door opened and the highest ranking officer in the compound, Chief Officer Li, stepped out. Approaching Robert, he welcomed him kindly and asked in a friendly tone, "When we handcuffed you, why were you smiling?"

Robert answered, "First of all, I believe in God. Second, I trust in the law, and third, I trust myself."

With the same friendly voice, Chief Officer Li asked, "Which church do you belong to?"

Robert proudly replied, "The Seventh-day Adventists."

Then the chief officer asked him if he was familiar with a man named Chung Fei-long.

Robert surmised that Chief Officer Li hoped he would become a Judas, betraying Christians into the government's hands. Providing such information would give him merit with the guards and perhaps even secure him an early release. But at what cost? Did he want to be responsible for the arrests of other Christians? He determined that as long as he could help it, he would never reveal any information that might cause another to suffer; he would answer only for himself. Like Abram, when Pharaoh asked if Sarai was his wife, Robert told a half-truth when he was questioned about Chung Fei-long. Choosing his words carefully, he replied, "I'm not familiar with him." Bothered by his conscience because of his deception, he vainly tried to assuage his guilt through mind games. He did *know of* the man, but he did not really know him, at least, not at a familiar level.

Chung Fei-long was the father of one of Robert's classmates in the academy. He was also working with an American named Elder E. L. Longway, the former president of the China Division of Seventh-day Adventists, who had subsequently become a missionary in Hong Kong. Elder Longway had been sending food to Chung to be distributed to the needy, which was technically illegal. That was about the extent of Robert's knowledge about Mr. Chung. Were he to tell what he knew, Chief Officer Li would never understand. From the officer's standpoint, many of those needy people had been selected by local authorities for punishment as counterrevolutionaries. Not a few of them were Christians. Others were beggars who had fallen through the cracks of Mao's promised bamboo rice bowl. No doubt, Chief Officer Li, like so many others in positions of authority, wouldn't want to hear about holes in the system. Therefore, Robert self-righteously concluded, it was none of the officer's business. *Under the circumstances,* Robert thought, as he tried to justify in his own mind his attempt to deceive, *the less said, the better.*

After hearing the answer to his second question, Chief Officer Li left, clearly disappointed. New guards replaced the ones who had arrested him. Stepping into the Number One detention building, Robert noticed an impressive slogan in huge black Chinese characters on a white wall. It declared, "Leniency to those who freely confess their crimes and severity to those who refuse." Robert thought the prison rule somewhat paralleled God's plan of salvation. Anyone who sought forgiveness through Jesus Christ would receive it, but those who stubbornly refused to accept His grace would be punished in the final judgment.

Mind Games

On another wall was a list of prison rules. He had little time to read all of them as he was marched down the hall, but he noticed a few Chinese characters that stated, "Subject to discipline: Cannot speak or act carelessly. If you want something, first get approval from an officer or guard. Do not exchange name, address, or any details of your case. If you see anyone violating these rules, report the offense to a guard. Keep the daily schedule strictly. Do not fight. Confess your crimes thoroughly. Study Chairman Mao's work diligently to reform yourself."

As he was checked in, the guards thoroughly searched his belongings, confiscating whatever they wished. Pulling out the pocket Bible Robert's family had lovingly packed, they confiscated it. Sadness struck him as he realized he would need to survive in prison without the Word of God.

After processing him, the guards issued him a prison number. "Don't forget this number," they advised. "You no longer have a name! Don't ever use it again. From now on, Criminal 153, you're just a number." The number seemed familiar. Robert remembered that in the Chinese hymnal it was the song, "All the Way My Savior Leads Me," and he felt comforted. His Savior would certainly lead him all the way through whatever lay ahead.

Handing Robert a copy of Chairman Mao's Little Red Book of political and social sayings, a guard commanded, "Study this, 153! It teaches you how to fit into New China. Might get you out of here sooner!" Picking up a newspaper, he added, "Each morning you'll have twenty minutes to read today's copy of the *Liberation Daily*, Shanghai's number-one newspaper. One of you will read it aloud to the rest of you. When time's up, it will be taken away. The next day we'll give you a new issue."

Two police officers cut the zippers off Robert's jacket and trousers and took away his shoe laces. Then they ordered him to read the prison rules painted on the wall. When Robert acknowledged that he was acquainted with them, two police officers led him upstairs to a maximum security center reserved for cultural revolutionaries like him. In the dim light he saw iron bars and a long gray corridor with rows of cells, each with a heavy brown door. A chilling wind blew through the hall, making Robert shiver. He was showed into a cell, and the door was shut and locked behind him. Examining his surroundings, he counted nine fellow inmates, each with his head shaven.

After staring at Robert for some time, one inmate exclaimed, "You're lucky!" Before Robert could reply, the cellmate explained, "You've still got your hair. Your case must be minor. As long as you've got your hair, you won't stay long! We got shaved when they checked us in, so we'll be here awhile, but you—your crime must be minor. You may be out in a few months!"

"How long have you been here?" Robert asked.

"We've lost track."

"How do you spend your time?"

"There is nothing much to do. In the beginning we passed the time by counting the days on our fingers, hoping we would be out in a matter of days. When we ran out of fingers, we counted the weeks, then the months. For a while we counted the years. Soon the days themselves wore on like years, and we stopped counting. That was after our heads were shaved bald. We don't have much hope. But you do! You still have a full head of hair, so don't worry. You won't stay long. In this prison, it's very easy to get in, but almost impossible to get out. One of us, after getting his head shaved, has been waiting over ten years just to have his case reviewed. He's never been charged and never been sentenced. But you are different." The inmate smiled broadly. "You have hair, so you have hope."

Robert wondered why his head had not been shaved. Was he truly better off than the others? Or was it just another mind game? Were they giving him false hope? Or was his hair spared in an attempt to weaken the resolve of his cellmates?

The other prisoners sat with their backs along the brick wall of a cell that Robert guessed was about nine feet wide by twelve feet long. The center of the cell was bare, with no tables, chairs, or beds. The inmates would need that floor space to lie on at night. Robert sat on the wooden floor. The room became as quiet as an empty tomb.

Soon he heard the tread of approaching feet. The window to the cell opened, and someone called his number. When he responded, the voice replied, "Follow me."

Mind Games

The cell door opened. Pushing himself off the floor, Robert followed the guard down a hall to a room with a wooden chair. He was told to sit.

He did not have to wait long. Carrying important looking documents in their hands, a panel of inquisitors filed in and sat down, facing him. Under Chinese law, an arrested man is assumed guilty until he can prove himself innocent. Panel members fired questions at him related to proselytizing and spying, and he answered. His accusers declared, "We know your crimes, so confess! Tell us now, and we will be lenient." Often members of the panel would let him see a corner of one of their papers, just so he would know that they "knew." However, Robert noticed that they never let him read very carefully anything they offered him, which suggested to Robert that, in reality, they had no evidence against him. Perhaps that explained why he still had his hair.

Suddenly, almost disconcertingly, the panel arose, and the guard escorted Robert back to his cell. He returned to his spot on the floor, sat, and waited.

CHAPTER 9

Sitting Until the Floor Rots

As he sat on the polished wooden floor waiting for his next interview, Robert had one consolation: his full head of hair. If his cellmates were right, he would be out of prison soon.

Days and weeks went by. Then, almost three months after he had been placed in detention, Christmas came—his first Christmas in jail. It was a Christmas he would never forget. The guard chose Christmas Day to lead the prisoners down the hall to the prison barber. Robert watched as his fellow inmates got their heads shaved. Then, when it was his turn to have his hair cut, he noticed the guard whispering to the barber while giving Robert a sly look. Intuitively, Robert discerned what it meant. Even though there was no mirror in the room, as the barber snipped away, he understood what was happening. Seeing the length of the strands piled on the floor, he knew his hair was gone, and with it his hope for an early release. The shaved head was intended to be both humiliating and demoralizing.

He saw the guard looking at him intently, watching for his reaction and recalled that, in earlier months, some prisoners had sobbed bitterly when they were shaved. For prisoners, a man's hair is his glory; to many, being deprived of it is a serious affront. Afraid that he might reveal his feelings, Robert resisted the urge to stroke his head. He had no need to confirm that he was bald. Definitely he was. Allowing the guard to watch him run his hand over his smooth scalp would give the guard more satisfaction than he deserved. Looking down again at the pile of hair on the cement, he remembered O. Henry's Christmas story, "The Gift of the Magi," and thought about the heroine's beautiful long hair. She had sold her hair to buy an accessory for her husband's prize watch. She had cut her hair to buy a Christmas present for the one she loved.

That, he realized, was what he had done. He had given his hair as a Christmas present for Jesus.

Silently he prayed, "My beloved Lord, You were born in a manger and died on a cross for me. I love you so much for what you have done. I offer my hair and my heart to you this Christmas. With a smile, I will hold my head high." And with that, Robert walked away, his head held high. Inwardly he felt honored. His shaven head was a symbol that now he was truly a prisoner for Christ like Peter and Paul. He told himself, any suffering he was bound to endure was nothing in comparison to Christ's agony. He would accept the cup of suffering if that was God's will for his life. He prayed that God would keep him strong in his future trials.

****

Over the next few months, Robert was called in sporadically for questioning. Sometimes he would be called in several days in a row; other times he would be ignored for months. The irregularity of his interviews was one of the mind games played by the guards. For a time, he would feel like he was making progress, when, all the while, he suspected that they were hoping to trip him up under the intensity of their frequent inquisitions. Perhaps they wanted him to say something he would later regret. Most likely they were wearing him down, hoping to persuade him to offer them information they wanted to hear—anything that they could use against him. At other times, the feeling that they were letting him rot made him despair that his case would ever be resolved. Being left alone, Robert knew, was yet another psychological game played by the guards in the hope that, in desperation, he would tell them anything they wanted him to say.

PRISONER FOR CHRIST

To keep from falling into melancholy, Robert exercised his mind. In the enforced silence, he had plenty of time to think. He prayed almost ceaselessly, meditated, and quoted Bible verses, reciting in particular from the books of Daniel and Revelation. Reviewing Daniel's prophecies and interpreting them helped his mental state. When he wasn't doing that, he obediently read the political pages of Chairman Mao's Little Red Book or analyzed details from the conversations he had had with his inquisitors.

Once, he recalled, an inquisitor had said, "It's very hot today. I've been where something is cool. I just ate some cool food. A Tianjin bun." Robert could almost picture the famous cold dish from Tianjin, a city near the national capital of Beijing. His mouth began watering. Almost as if the inquisitor had known how Robert was feeling, he had shattered the spell by continuing his line of questioning. "When I was there, I met this old guy." He hadn't said the man's name, but Robert guessed that he was talking about the Seventh-day Adventist union president, who lived in Tianjin. "Have you met him?" the inquisitor asked.

"Only once," Robert had replied. It was the truth. The union president's daughter had come to Shanghai once. Robert had visited her.

"What were his orders to you?"

"He gave me no orders," Robert said. "We shook hands, and that's all." So, Robert surmised, they were looking for a vast Christian conspiracy. He thought he had answered well that time. Reviewing the situation, he renewed his vow that, with God's help, he would never report the activities of others.

Soon another conversation came to mind. "Your father's dead," the inquisitor had stated rhetorically. "It seems that he died in the fifties. You preach the resurrection, don't you? Now, prisoner 153, if your father were alive today, I would believe in Jesus." Seeing an opportunity to witness to his instructor, Robert had explained to him that, in fact, he did not believe that his father was alive at the present time. Rather, he believed that he would be raised to life at the sound of the last trumpet, when every eye will see Jesus appear the second time. Analyzing that conversation, Robert shook his head inwardly. Where had that inquisitor learned about the resurrection?

Sitting Until the Floor Rots

On a deeper plane, Robert saw that, by making light of the resurrection, they had hoped to plant seeds of doubt so that he could give up his religion. It was a mind game Robert refused to play. Instead, he resolved that, with Christ's help, he would stand up for what he believed even though the heavens fell around him. He would never deny his Savior.

The sound of feet came toward the cell. Sliding the window open, a guard called, "Criminal 153!" Responding, Robert followed the guard to the inquisition room.

The panel filed in. Confidently one of them asserted, "China is strong ideologically and militarily. Give up your fancy ideas. Russia won't help you, and Chiang Kai-shek isn't coming back!"

Robert understood immediately what was behind the statement. Earlier he and the other inmates had been supplied with newspapers. In 1964, Chairman Mao and the Communist Party were at their height. Recent headlines had boasted that China had developed an atomic bomb and that Russian party chairman Nikita Khrushchev had been dethroned. Unlike the days of the Korean War, China no longer needed to fear either America or Russia. Clearly China's propaganda machine had intensified its agenda.

The remark about Russia was quite revealing. It referred to an earlier interview when Robert had tried to encourage tolerance toward him by suggesting to his inquisitors that China could learn from Russia, which, under Khrushchev, allowed a degree of religious freedom. It also meant that his remark about Russia was a stain in his dossier that had come back to haunt him.

Robert remembered reading the news in his cell. Khrushchev's fall and China's atomic bomb had made headlines in the *Liberation Daily*, the local newspaper. He couldn't help thinking that Satan delights in magnifying the world's power to intimidate God's people as he did when he drove Goliath to challenge Israel. But Robert knew that God's children have a different view of worldly greatness. In Proverbs 16:18, Solomon declared that "pride goeth before destruction." The rule applied to everyone—popes, presidents, Nebuchadnezzar, Belshazzar, Hitler, and now Khrushchev. Khrushchev had once boasted that Russia would change the Christian era. The year 1917 would mark the first year of the new human epoch. Russian cosmonauts, after circling the earth, sent back the message, "We haven't found God out here." Now Khrushchev had fallen from power just as the proverb had predicted. Generations pass, but God is eternal. Man had made a great issue out of the cosmonaut's assertions, but God enabled Robert's mind to remain stable. Having analyzed the Russian situation, Robert decided it was the better part of wisdom to keep his thoughts to himself at the moment. He turned his thoughts to Taiwan.

The snide remark about the impossibility of Chiang Kai-shek returning reflected China's insistence that when Christians said they awaited the return of Jesus, they really meant they longed for the Nationalists to return from Taiwan and overthrow the Communists. The accusation also showed the government's relief that it no longer needed to fear civil war.

Seeing that Robert had nothing to say, the panel member continued. "We have won ideologically and militarily, so, Criminal 153, give up your God! Communism will spread throughout the world. Soon every nation will fly China's red flag!"

Robert saw in that statement that China thought that she was more ideologically pure than her rival, Russia, which she considered to have fallen by the socialist wayside. The rise and fall of Khrushchev only confirmed her position: The Russian bear was no longer really Communist. China thought she alone would carry on Communism's hegemonic aim of spreading true Marxism around the globe.

Would China's red flag fly over every nation? Robert thought not. The second chapter of Daniel came to mind. He could almost see the statue in Nebuchadnezzar's dream towering over him. The feet of iron and clay gave him the answer to China's intense propaganda. How could China unite the world under Communism when God had told Daniel that the feet of iron and clay could never mix? No matter how hard China tried, it was clear to Robert that never again would there be a country ruling the world, as had the so-called global empires of the ancient world. Therefore, he concluded, China's red flag could never fly over every nation of the world.

Turning to the panel, Robert said triumphantly, "I will never give up my God!"

The door opened, and a guard led Robert back to his cell, where he sat and returned to his mental exercises. Soon he recalled a couple of other interviews that represented another category of mind games the panel liked to play. In the first of these interviews, a panel member had asked, "Do you have an old mother?"

"Yes."

"Do you want to see her again?"

"I have repeatedly asked for permission to write to my mother," Robert said boldly. "But I've never been allowed to send any messages to her yet. When can I post her a letter?"

Without answering his question directly, the panel member retorted, "If you want to see her again, tell us what we want."

Robert did not reply. He refused to fall into their trap and confess to crimes he had not committed. Obviously the guards had no evidence against him.

The face of the investigator grew livid. Angrily striking the table with his fist, he exploded with a string of abuse. "Young fellow!" he threatened, "you don't know how high the sky is or how deep is the earth. Rein in your stubborn horse before it falls off a precipice. What kind of place do you think this is? We have tape recordings of interviews with other prisoners. Would you like to hear them? I've already faced a man far more stubborn than you! Where is he now? If you want to see your mother again, answer our questions. If you insist on going your own way, sit on the floor until it wears out. Or would you rather see your mother? Now go to your cell and consider."

Robert was not called for another interview for three months. He felt as though he had been sealed in a box and shelved indefinitely.

One night, lying in his corner soon after that explosive interview, Robert dreamed of his mother with gray hair. She seemed so near. Then the words of the interrogator rang in his ears. "If you insist on going your own way, you will sit on the floor until it wears out! Or would you rather see your mother again?" Robert remembered telling his mother not to cry on the day of his arrest. There on the floor of his cell, tears welled up in his own eyes. He thought, *I comforted my mother, but who will comfort me?* He turned his face to the wall, hoping to hide his emotions from the others. "God, I reveal my weakness only to you," he prayed.

The next day, after lunch, the police had lined up the inmates to take a walk inside the jail. Still struggling with the thought that he might never see his mother again, Robert had not been in the mood for exercise. Dragging his feet, he had followed the others reluctantly. Suddenly a line from a hymn came to mind: "Jesus' love is more than maternal love."[1] The words strengthened him. Try as he might, though, the rest of the hymn eluded him. He could remember only those first few words. Singing them softly as he paced behind his cellmates, his heart gradually grew warm. Once again he entrusted himself and his family to Jesus.

After having no interview for three months, Robert was called in again and told that his sister had visited him. "She left you a letter." A guard handed it to him. It was a simple letter. "Do you want to see her again and read her letters?" the guard asked.

"Of course I do," Robert said and then coughed. He had suffered a bout of tuberculosis before and wondered if it was returning.

"Then you consider," the guard said knowingly after hearing Robert's cough. "You have been advised. Tell us everything. Now go back to your cell," the guard yelled. "Sit on the floor until it rots!"

Sitting on the floor, contemplating that conversation, it became clear to Robert that they wanted him to lose his mind or feel dependent upon them for social interaction. Talk between fellow inmates was forbidden. He could talk only when the authorities called him in for questioning. By saying he could wait until the floor rotted, they meant they would wait patiently until he gave in to their requests. By depriving him of his family, they were hoping he would give in and confess whatever they wanted him to say. Right then and there, Robert made his third resolve. He would never give in to their wishes.

As the number of days in the cell multiplied, he rejoiced that God was teaching him something about the last judgment. Robert recalled that the Bible states that just before the end of probation, Jesus would examine the record of each person and decide whether he was righteous or filthy. At that time, no one besides Jesus could represent him. Likewise, while he was in the Number One Detention Block, no human being could answer for him. When he felt depressed, he reminded himself that his number was 153—"All the Way My Savior Leads Me." Though he had to answer seemingly alone, his Savior was always with him.

Sitting Until the Floor Rots

Refusing to give out information about others, give up his faith, or give in to their demands, he fought the guards' mind games as best he could, though he at times succumbed to practicing deception. Strengthened by his three weapons—prayer, meditation, and Scripture—Robert rested in the knowledge that if he were faithful, God would grant him eternal life. Therefore, Robert thought, even if his tuberculosis returned and he died in prison, time was on his side. If, to be released, he had to sit until the floor rotted beneath him, he could wait.

---

[1] Later Robert learned that the line was from hymn 68 in the Chinese hymnal.

CHAPTER 10

Learning Patience

One wall of Robert's cell had an "X-ray window," as the inmates called it. It had a curtain on the other side which only the guards could open. The cellmates could not see out, but they knew the guards could see in. For reasons unknown to the prisoners, the curtain was usually shut. However, whenever the guards were watching, they opened the curtain—which served as a warning to follow prison rules.

Often the guards informed the prisoners of new rules only after an inmate had broken them. Occasionally prisoners were required to unlearn old rules—at their own expense—when no one had informed them that the rules had changed. A few rules seemed to remain constant. Prisoners were required to sit quietly on the wooden floor in their assigned spot and study the sayings of Chairman Mao to reform themselves. Paper and writing utensils were provided upon request to prisoners who wished to confess their crimes or wanted to report the crimes of others. Letters to the world outside the prison had to be read and approved by the guards. No letter could exceed one hundred Chinese characters. Robert's repeated requests to write to his family had been consistently denied. Each inmate was expected to take a turn cleaning the cell. Because Robert shared his cell with eight or nine others, his cleaning duty came once every nine or ten days. No one could exercise unless ordered to do so by the guards. Generally, exercising involved lining up single file and walking along the cell walls until commanded to return to their spots. Any deviance from these rules would be punished. Creativity was promptly squelched.

One of Robert's cellmates, a young man who had barely graduated from college, grew bored. Being creative, he whittled a sewing needle out of a piece of wood.

Eyeing what the young college graduate was making, a guard burst into the cell, grabbed the needle and yelled, "Don't ever do that again!" With that, he placed the young man's hands behind his back and handcuffed them. "Read Chairman Mao's sayings instead," he ordered. As the guard left, he promised, "I'll release you in twenty-four hours."

The next day, the poor young graduate could not eat, drink, or relieve himself easily, let alone read, because his hands were behind his back, and no one volunteered to help. The young man was accustomed to sleeping on his back, and Robert noticed that the young man got very little sleep that night.

When the appointed time arrived, no one came to the cell. Had the guard broken his promise on purpose? Robert wondered. Or had he just forgotten? The college graduate waited another day and well into a third, but still the guard did not return. He looked more and more uncomfortable.

Suddenly, another guard looked in through the sliding window. "Exercise time," he announced. "Stand up, walk around the room. Stay close to the walls. Make rounds until I tell you to stop. Hurry! Hurry!"

The cellmates obeyed instantly. Even if their muscles were partially atrophied, making it difficult to take the first few wobbly steps, they preferred walking to sitting. Robert quickly snapped into line. Suddenly, the hand-cuffed young graduate stopped following, stood at the cell door, and frantically banged his head against it. His pounding grew louder and louder until the door opened and guards filed in. After the exercise routine had been halted, the entire group was escorted down the hall to the inquisition room.

When everyone was situated, the guard called out Robert's prisoner number. "Criminal 153, report!"

Thinking quickly, Robert considered the risks to both the young man and himself; then, despite the fact that he might arouse the wrath of at least one of the guards, he decided to talk straight. Looking directly into the guard's eyes, he spoke with authority. "If you want to know why this young college graduate was hitting his head against the wall, ask yourselves what you've done. Let me explain. A few days ago a guard caught this young graduate whittling a piece of wood into a sewing needle. After ordering him never to carve wood again, he placed him in handcuffs, promising to release him the next day. For twenty-four hours, it was hard for this young graduate to read Chairman Mao, or to eat, or to drink, or to sleep, or even to relieve himself, but he took his punishment manfully, knowing it would end at a certain time. Then, when the time came for him to be released, the guard did not come. The young man waited another twenty-four hours and then grew impatient. I admit that was wrong. Patience is a virtue. But one of the guards caused him to become impatient by breaking a promise."

The guards were speechless.

Immediately, one of them removed the young college graduate's handcuffs, whereupon, without another word, all the prisoners were ordered to file up and return to their cell. Unceremoniously, the young college graduate was escorted to the hospital.

As he sat back in his place on the floor, Robert suspected that he had created an enemy, one who would keep a close eye on him. One who had the power to get even with him for exposing an error. But Robert was glad that he could help an inmate. Perhaps his cellmates would see that Christians are different from other people. Maybe they would think Christians care. Would any of them want to learn about his God?

****

Next to Robert sat a man whose facial features were arabesque, which told Robert that he was most likely from Xinjiang Province, the area where Mary, Robert's girlfriend, had once worked. Likely he was a Uygur, a member of a minority tribe in that area. How his neighbor had come to Shanghai from Xinjiang was a mystery.

Learning Patience

Robert guessed that the Uygur had been arrested for his belief in Islam.

Despite the rule that inmates were to keep silent, Robert tried to talk with his nearest cellmate whenever he had a chance. Reading Chairman Mao's book had become boring. How many times can a person read a book before it is committed to memory? Any intellectual challenge on its pages had long since vanished. Yet reading it remained mandatory. He read it only to find useful sayings that he could quote in his defense when questioned by a guard.

Then an idea came to him. Turning to his Muslim neighbor, he asked, "Can you teach me the Uygur alphabet?"

The Uygur's face lit up. Taking some paper, Robert opened his Little Red Book, placed the paper inside, and then passed the book to his cellmate. Carefully, the Uygur wrote some squiggly lines and dots that made up part of the Uygur alphabet and then returned the book to him. Robert pretended to study Mao's sayings while actually learning to write the Uygur alphabet. Both men found the experience far more enjoyable than reading Chairman Mao.

All went well until one day the curtain opened as the Uygur was teaching his language to Robert.

Moments later the cell door opened and in stomped the guard who had handcuffed the young whittler. Grabbing Mao's book from Robert's hand, he opened it and took out the paper covered with lines, squiggles, and dots. "What's this?" he asked.

"The Uygur alphabet—one of the written languages of a Chinese minority from Xinjiang," Robert replied.

"You shouldn't be learning this!" barked the guard.

"Why not?" Robert asked. "Take out a renminbi note. You'll see that the Uygur language is written on our money."

"You shouldn't give the other prisoners a bad example." Not wanting to be confused by facts, the guard was obviously gloating because at long last he could find some fault with Robert. "If the others see that you're not reading Mao," he continued, "they won't read him either. Think of your influence." With that, he jerked Robert's arms behind his back and snapped on a pair of handcuffs. "I'll release you in twenty hours," he snorted, marching out triumphantly.

For the next twenty hours, Robert could not eat, drink, or relieve himself. Fortunately, after seeing how he had defended the young whittler, some of the inmates helped him. Uncomfortable though it was, he managed to lie on his side and catch some sleep.

To Robert's joy, this time the guard kept his promise, returning after exactly twenty hours to remove the handcuffs. Clearly, thought Robert, the guard had learned his lesson.

Sitting in his cell, reflecting, Robert considered the incident carefully, wondering why God had let it happen. Had God granted him an opportunity to gain empathy for others? Despite the thought that the guard had punished him out of spite, he thanked God for giving him a lesson in patience. Recalling the guard's prediction that if he were to remain stubborn, he would sit on the floor until it rotted away, Robert realized that his time in handcuffs had given him considerable insight into how firm the floor really was and how long it might take for the floor to rot. Undoubtedly, in the days and weeks and months to come, he would learn more about patience.

CHAPTER 11

Cleaning Up

With the exception of an occasional interview concerning Robert's case and the rotation of cleaning duty, the daily prison routine between 1964 and 1968 soon blurred into a monotonous sameness. Investigation into his case was dropped indefinitely in mid-1965, terminating the interviews that had once broken the boredom. Without the investigations, prisoners found it more difficult to keep track of the days. But Robert found a way. He determined time by keeping a close watch on the cleaning rotation. Based on seat numbers, each inmate was required to take a daily turn cleaning their twelve-foot by nine-foot room and the toilet.

Depending on the number of prisoners in the cell, an inmate cleaned perhaps once in ten days. Prisoners were frequently transferred into or out of a cell, constantly altering the number of inmates. Sometimes, Robert might find himself cleaning once in seventeen days. When the cell was especially crowded, it was once in twenty days. Robert himself was occasionally transferred to another cell. Whenever he was placed in a new cell, his seat number changed, which forced him to recalculate the days. And then there were transfers to the hospital to treat his resurgent tuberculosis, making his efforts to determine the day of the week even more challenging. Despite all these changes, Robert managed.

If, as was usually the case, his cleaning duty came on a weekday, he always cleaned; but he sought to make a difference on Sabbath.

One day, Robert calculated that his next turn to clean would fall on Sabbath. He had recently been transferred, so he had never needed to ask any favors of his new cellmates. He planned carefully. Making such a request of his neighbor was dangerous. Because talking was forbidden, if a guard heard him, he would be in trouble. Refusing to clean for religious reasons would give his cellmates an opportunity to gain merit by reporting him. Still, he knew he had to take the risk.

On Friday, when he felt certain that the guards were on the other side of the prison, he turned to the inmate on his left, who Robert knew was not a Christian, and whispered, "Can you clean for me tomorrow? I'll clean up the next day for you."

"What's the matter?" The inmate showed concern as he answered softly. "Are you not feeling well?" Occasionally, the symptoms of Robert's tuberculosis would become apparent, and he would be taken to the hospital.

After listening to be sure the footfall of the guard was distant, Robert replied, "I feel fine."

"Then why can't you clean tomorrow?" The inmate looked puzzled.

Smiling, Robert explained. "I'm a Christian, and as a Christian I celebrate the Sabbath. Tomorrow is the seventh day of the week, which is my Sabbath. Six days are for us. On those days we can work and follow our own pleasure, but God taught us to rest on the seventh day and give it to Him. I spend the time communicating with my Savior, Jesus Christ."

"So you're a Christian?"

Robert nodded ever so slightly. "Would you clean for me tomorrow? I'm not afraid of work. I'll gladly take your shift when it's your turn."

When the inmate did not respond immediately, Robert hastily added, "If it's a problem, I'll just ask my friend on my right. Perhaps I can trade with him."

"It's no problem," the inmate replied.

"Good. Thank you. I'll clean for you on Sunday then." And so it was agreed. Robert felt good that he could use cleaning as a subtle means to witness. It enabled him to tell his cellmates that he was an Adventist Christian.

True to his word, the next day, Robert's neighbor cleaned. Undoubtedly some noticed, but because talking was forbidden, no one commented. The prisoners piled their meager belongings in a corner and withdrew to another corner while the room was cleaned. Several minutes later, when the floor had been wiped, the prisoners grabbed their belongings and returned to their seats with them. The cleaner wiped where the pile had been and sat down in his place.

Sunday, when it should have been his neighbor's cleaning day, Robert replaced him. With what remained from the water provided to wash his face, he wet his prison towel. The other prisoners gathered their belongings in the daily routine.

During his four years in the detention houses awaiting trial, Robert had no trouble keeping Sabbath. He always asked a neighbor to exchange with him. Usually, no one refused. If one did, he always asked the inmate on the other side. One of them always helped.

Fortunately for Robert, none of the guards ever noticed, and no one ever reported. For this, Robert praised God and thanked Him for opportunities to witness.

CHAPTER 12

The Mysterious Cross on the Door

The morning whistle blew. Robert and his cellmates arose hurriedly. Tired and listless, they straightened their bedclothes on the floor and set their respective areas in order. Once everything was prepared, they awaited the water ration. Soon an attendant thrust a hose through the panel window, and each prisoner filled his basin with a quart of water. This they would have to use for bathing, for washing clothes, for brushing teeth, and for cleaning the cell. Shortly afterward, a hose appeared and each received about a quart of boiled water for drinking.

Breakfast, dispensed in aluminum boxes, came next. The menu of rice porridge with a few salted vegetables never changed. The inmate on duty received and divided the vegetables. Then everyone rose, formed a circle in the middle of the cell, and played a finger game called *mora* to determine who got the pickle that day.

To play the game, the prisoners counted; then, at the right instant, each quickly shot out one of three choices: two fingers for scissors, a fist for a rock or five fingers for cloth. Winners would be determined on the following basis: the scissors cut the cloth, the rock broke the scissors and the cloth captured the rock. The players tried to guess what their opponents would select and chose the stronger weapon or the same one as their opponent. Then at least they could play again.

The Mysterious Cross on the Door

Having joined with the others, Robert awaited his turn. As they played around the circle the one who lost stepped out and the winner turned to the next prisoner. Perhaps he would win another round, or he would need to step out. Eventually, the prisoner beside Robert turned, they counted, and Robert shot out two fingers; but his opponent produced a fist. Robert returned to his seat. Someone else ate the pickle that day.

Though the finger game seemed like too much fun to any passing guard—who generally growled at the players if he happened to observe the activity—it prevented needless squabbles. When all was settled, everyone—except the newcomers—ate with great relish. When one is on the verge of starvation, even the blandest food gets gobbled up. Before taking his first bite, Robert made it his habit to visibly ask for a blessing on his food. He did so not just as a form of witness, but because the way the food tasted, it needed to be blessed! For most self-respecting Chinese, good manners required that one not be bothered with the last sip in one's bowl. But when all the prisoners had finished eating, much to Robert's bewilderment at first, one of them collected the boxes and, with his fingers, drew up a mouthful of the remaining rice water and swallowed it. The longer Robert remained in prison, however, the more he became acquainted with hunger himself. Soon nothing that occurred at mealtime seemed out of place to him.

Though it was against the rules to talk, whenever the prisoners thought they could get away with it, they did. A favorite topic of conversation was food and how to prepare it. Feeding on illusions, they were visualizing cake to allay hunger. Robert noted that as terrible as it was to suffer hunger, starvation of the mind was far worse. The inmates fell mentally or spiritually ill first, and then their physical strength disintegrated.

At the appointed time, a guard delivered the local newspaper, the *Liberation Daily*, for twenty minutes. One of the inmates read it aloud while the others listened. Occasionally, the guard would forget to retrieve it. Then, even though they suspected the newspaper had been left for propaganda purposes, the prisoners devoured each character on every page.

Once, Robert saw a piece of yellowed newspaper drop from the window. The police covered the outside windows with paper, and a corner of the newspaper on that window had somehow been torn off and fallen to the floor inside the cell. Others saw it too. Instantly, several cellmates rushed for it, throwing themselves onto the floor in an attempt to grab it. So desperate were they for mental stimulation, they struggled for it at great risk for, not only was the reading material forbidden, but no prisoner was permitted to fight.

Paper and pens were not available unless an inmate wished to confess his crimes or to report on a cellmate. After one made a confession, he *might* be allowed to keep his pen and any leftover paper, but the chances were slim. Robert soon realized that intellectually and emotionally, he was living on a desert island.

The desolation of Robert's cell decreased for him one day when, just before lunch, the heavy door opened and a new prisoner came in. His hair had not yet been cut. When he sat down in the corner, Robert gazed at him for a while. After the newcomer took his food box, he did not eat in a hurry like the others.

After lunch, the guard ordered the prisoners to line up and walk along the cell walls. Generally at this time, the prisoners could talk with each other. Often Robert would croon a hymn. This time he hummed because he thought he might have seen the newcomer praying. Hoping he was a Christian, Robert thought it worth the gamble.

As he walked, Robert noticed that the newcomer was trying to get close to him. When he caught up, he followed close behind and hummed the same tune. With that response, Robert felt certain that the newcomer was indeed a Christian and a potential friend with whom he could share ideas.

Though the prisoners were forbidden to exchange names or information about their cases, the newcomer told Robert his English name was Adam. In time, Robert discovered that Adam was blind in one eye and that the other eyelid closed whenever he smiled. Happily, Robert learned such a smile was frequently expressed. Later he found out that Adam was a faithful Christian and an active worker in his church. One of his friends had been Robert's music teacher in the seminary. Adam himself had been a civil engineer before his arrest. Because of his social relationships and having visited church members, he had become suspect. Unfortunately, one of his conversations was betrayed by a Judas in his church. He was separated from his family for a month and was beaten and kicked, which resulted in a damaged kidney and hematuria. Eventually the police had arrested him and sent him to Robert's cell in the Number One Detention Center. As Adam sat near him, Robert could see that Adam's feet were still swollen. Robert observed that, despite all this, he was a joyful character. Other inmates also noticed Adam's cheer and often commended him.

Once, when the guards were beyond earshot, the one-eyed engineer told Robert, "I'm like Nicodemus because I'm unable to show my religion openly. But I still keep the faith."

Whenever the guards announced it was exercise time and the prisoners marched around in their cell, if Adam went forward, Robert followed. To avert suspicion, sometimes Robert went first followed by Adam.

As they exercised, most of the prisoners talked to make up for the long imposed silence while sitting. Sometimes Robert recited a Bible text just loud enough for Adam to hear. Adam would respond with a related verse. Then he might hum a spiritual song and Robert would echo it. Both rejoiced in each other's fellowship. Surely, they thought, God had appointed their rendezvous in Number One Detention Center. Their interactions renewed their strength.

One night, when the other prisoners were asleep, Adam quietly talked with Robert. "When I stayed in the cell next door, I found a large cross marked on the thick wooden door. As far as I could tell, it could have been there quite some time." Because they were afraid of being overpowered by the prisoners, the guards were afraid to set foot in that cell. "Probably that explains why that cross has never been discovered."

"Let me tell you a story," Robert spoke softly. Adam was eager to listen. "Two months before you arrived, I met another young man. When he saw me praying every day, he secretly let me know that he was interested in Christianity. His mother was studying the Bible in a pastor's home. The young man somehow got involved in a political discussion and was arrested. In prison, he prayed with me every morning. He also asked me to tell him more Bible truths and wanted me to write some verses for him."

"That's a most dangerous undertaking," said Adam.

"But how could I refuse a friend who knocked at the door of my heart asking for bread?"

"What did you do?" As the one-eyed engineer smiled, his good eye closed.

"I secretly wrote down texts like the twenty-third psalm on a piece of tissue paper."

"Did he report you?"

"No," Robert replied. "He kept it in Mao's Little Red Book."

"The only reading material allowed," Adam beamed.

"While others slept, he took out the book and, under the faint light of that fifteen-watt bulb over there, studied it tirelessly." They smiled at each other. "Occasionally—" Robert coughed and then continued, "someone had a sleepless night, saw him reading, and ridiculed him, saying something like, 'How progressive he is! It's too late now. If he'd read Mao before, he probably wouldn't have been arrested!' Ridicule him they did, but nobody dared to prevent him from openly learning what they mistakenly believed were Mao's writings. In that way, deceitful though it is, he was free to read the Bible texts on a piece of toilet paper whenever he saw fit.

"That young man was quite a character." Robert went off on a tangent. "He was very active in the daytime. Whenever we got an opportunity to walk outside, he took advantage of the guard's inattention. He even exercised by performing handsprings and cartwheels. Once a policewoman saw him doing this and rebuked him, saying, 'Are you so happy, acting like a monkey?' "

The one-eyed engineer smiled infectiously.

"That reminds me of another incident about this young man that is worth reporting." Robert continued his story, this time following his tangent in a different direction. "Once, a cellmate was given boiling water in a wash basin. As he held the basin up to the window, the guard poured in the boiling water with a ladle, filling the basin to the brim and scalding the poor inmate's hands. Dropping the basin, he spilled the water. It spread all over the floor and onto our belongings, soaking our clothes and even the quilts that were piled over in that corner.

The Mysterious Cross on the Door

"The young man who sat near the door immediately took off his cotton-padded jacket and threw it on the floor to absorb the water. We all admired him for his unselfish act. I praised God that human goodness could still be found within our cell, despite our present condition. His act was especially admirable because of its corresponding risk." Adam nodded as he listened, knowing that drying a jacket was a problem. The guards forbade it. "To prevent him from being singled out for blame," Robert continued, "all of us caught his spirit and helped him hang up the jacket.

"Early the next morning, a guard looked through that so-called X-ray window and got a scare! At first he thought someone had hanged himself. Opening the panel on the door quickly, he shouted angrily, 'Who said you could hang that jacket up?' We told him what happened. After hearing the story, he commended the young man, saying, 'He's a good guy!' "

Hearing a noise, Robert fell silent, not knowing when he would get the chance to tell the rest of his story. Soon they were both asleep.

****

One day, after Adam had been through a series of investigations, he whispered to Robert, "Probably I'll be released before long. Would you like me to give any message to your family?"

Grateful for the chance, Robert began to think what to tell Adam and then decided to wait until news of the one-eyed engineer's release was more certain.

A few days later, the police called Adam's number and ordered him to collect his things. That meant he would be leaving. As he was packing, Robert seized the opportunity to tell him the conclusion to the story. "Remember the story I told you about the young man?" he quickly asked Adam. "I'm sure that that great cross was drawn on the door by him."

Then Adam surprised Robert by saying, "I think I met that man once in a friend's home. I didn't know anything about this at the time. Thank God and thank you!" Silently Robert thanked God and Adam for the sweet time they had shared in Christian fellowship.

Before Robert could give Adam a message for his family, guards appeared to escort Adam into solitary confinement. Prison policy dictated that, before a prisoner was released, he had to spend time in isolation. It made it more difficult for him to carry messages from the prisoners to the outside world.

After the one-eyed engineer left, Robert wanted to find out Adam's condition. During lunchtime, when the noise of the lunch boxes muffled voices, Robert called through the wall, "Adam! Adam!" Sadly, it seemed the lunch boxes were too loud, for Robert received no response. After a few days, Robert guessed that Adam had been released more quickly than even the one-eyed engineer himself had expected.

Shortly after Adam left, Robert himself was transferred to the smaller room where Adam had been before they'd met. Marked boldly upon the door was the cross Adam had described. Seeing it inspired Robert to leave small cross marks on the walls of other cells. As a mind game to preserve his sanity, Robert invented conversations he might have in heaven someday with individuals who had seen one of his crosses scribbled on the cell wall of a Shanghai prison. He imagined them saying something like, "Seeing that cross helped me to accept Christ."

CHAPTER 13

An Unexpected Temptation

In 1965, a document with twenty-three clauses was distributed even among the prisoners. It listed twenty-three prison practices that the government wanted reformed. Shortly afterward, the quality of the prison food improved, and the doors to the cells were left open. Robert noted that the majority of the bad elements like him—counterrevolutionaries—were being released. He wondered whether he dared hope his number would come up soon.

Because most of the prisoners remaining in his cell were not members of China's despised "intellectual" class, they could hardly read the writings of Chairman Mao. Robert, however, was accustomed to reading widely. One day he asked the guards if they could give him some books to read. "I don't care what books you give me," he said honestly. "I'll read anything you want me to read. Give me whatever you think will hasten my reform. I'll gladly read Marx, or even Lenin, if you have something written by them. Please give me some material to read in addition to Chairman Mao's Little Red Book." He reasoned he had nothing to lose. If he read the material they offered, he might gain merit and secure an early release. More important, reading would keep his mind active.

Shortly after Robert's request, Chief Officer Li—the same man whom he had met upon his arrival in the prison—came to his cell, called for Prisoner 153, opened the cell door and led him down the hall to his office. Closing the door, he showed Robert to a seat, sat across from him, and smiled broadly. "I've found the perfect solution to your case," he began.

Robert was all ears. Was he, at last, to learn about his court hearing and receive his sentence?

"I can arrange to have you released tomorrow, Criminal Huang. Your case can be cleared easily through me. After you're free, we'll give you a Seventh-day Adventist church to pastor and even allow you to conduct evangelistic programs. You can worship as you wish openly and freely without fear of ever being arrested again. This is all possible if you join the Party to help us now—secretly. No one will need to know you're our friend and helper except the two of us. What do you think about my idea?"

The offer was a total surprise. Robert was at a loss for words. Carefully, he analyzed the proposal before he answered. It seemed too good to be true! Was there a snag he had missed?

He recalled another day, years earlier, when he had been called to the office. The instructors had looked at him and said, "Your case is a difficult one. We cannot crack your crime. You must explain your crimes clearly to us." The impact of this request of the guard had not been lost upon Robert. In a legal system where one is guilty until proven innocent, this was about as close as the guard would come to admitting that they had no evidence against him. Most Chinese would confess crimes—whether real or imaginary—to please the authorities, but Robert was stubborn. He knew that if he offered no information, it couldn't be used against him. He was also *wai kiu*, which made him think somewhat differently. Unlike many Chinese, he understood English, which made a distinction between sins and crimes. The word in Chinese for sin is the same as the word for crime. As a minister it was his job to witness, which was a crime in China, but no sin against heaven. He had to obey God when man's laws conflicted with God's law. Because it appeared that the guards had no evidence that he was proselytizing, he had hoped for an early release. Robert had looked them in the eye and replied, "If you think I've done no crime, I have nothing to say."

An Unexpected Temptation

Bringing himself back to the present, he wondered, *Could it be that they are offering this solution because they don't know what to do with me, and this is a means by which they can save face? Why else would they offer me membership in the Party?*

Suddenly he realized their true intent. He recalled an evangelist in Shanghai who boldly conducted evangelistic meetings, yet the government left him alone. It had seemed so inconsistent. The Party forbade proselytizing, yet allowed this pastor's church to grow. After his death, high-ranking Party officials attended the funeral. That evangelist had been a secret Party member. No one had known he had joined—until the funeral. Then his church members guessed who had reported on them. Their pastor had been a spy for the Party. Often, after he baptized new members, some of the very members he had baptized had been arrested, while others disappeared—never to be seen or heard of again. How did that pastor live with himself? Robert wondered. Perhaps, in self-justification, he had reasoned that he had brought these people to Christ. If he didn't turn them in, someone else would. If they died believing in Jesus, their suffering would not be for naught, and he would have their stars on his crown. Or would he? Robert pondered. On whose side was he? Only God knew, Robert concluded.

If he took this offer, Robert knew he would be serving two masters. How could he serve God and the current atheistic regime bent on destroying Christianity? The Bible says man will either love one master or hate the other. Whom would he end up hating? To prove his loyalty to the Party, he would feel obligated to report his evangelistic activities, which could only be counterproductive. Certainly, if he did not report, his motives would become suspect, and he would be arrested again. The result would be the same as though he had never made a pact with them. Wouldn't it be better to evangelize in secret with no obligations? On the other hand, if he kept the authorities happy by keeping them informed, his double allegiance could be kept secret and perhaps he could bring more people to Jesus. But in time, perhaps at his funeral, his secret would be found out. Then what would his church members think? Would they doubt his teachings? Would they reject God because of him?

Looking Chief Officer Li in the eye, Robert graciously replied, "Thank you for trying to help me find an easy way out of here, but I cannot spy on my members and report their activities to you."

Chief Officer Li wiped the smile off his face. His polite tone vanished. "Then keep your foolish Christ!" he snarled. "An offer like mine is not made every day. You will live to regret your answer. Now, go back to your cell and sit on the floor until it rots!" Opening a door, he called for a guard, who escorted Robert back to his cell.

When Robert returned, the other prisoners were at a loss to know how to treat him. After seeing him taken away to talk with a chief official, they wondered whether he was a prisoner or a spy.

As the days ticked by, the inmates seemed to forget the incident.

CHAPTER 14

The Window of Heaven

One day during the lull in the prisoners' schedule between meal-time and the exercise routine, Robert listened carefully for the guards and then broke another prison rule. Standing up, he walked to the other side of the room and looked up toward the window in the wooden wall. There wasn't much to see unless he was unfortunate enough to see the eye of a guard! Indeed, it was the very same small window that the guards used to spy on the prisoners, but to Robert it became much more. To him, dangerous though it was, it was his window to the outside world—to heaven.

As discreetly as possible, he gazed upward and prayed silently. While he hoped that his witness might lead one inmate to ask him about God, he also felt a need to be careful. By praying so openly, he feared, someone might report him.

He was not the only one standing. Generally, others got up and walked around too. Wrapped in his prayer, Robert paid little attention to their activities.

Suddenly, hearing a guard approaching, Robert and the others dashed back to sit in their spaces. When the guard peeped through the window, everything was in order.

As the days wore on, Robert returned to his window as often as he thought it prudent to do. Like the proverbial window to heaven, it poured out spiritual strength that helped him maintain his sanity in a world gone awry. It transported him out of his cell into heaven. Heaven, where God saw and understood everything, even Robert and his plight.

Once in a while, Robert became so engrossed in prayer that he threw caution to the wind.

Peeking through the window one day, a guard saw Robert standing before it. Instantly, he called Robert's number, scolded him, handcuffed him, handed him a pen, and ordered, "Confess!" Writing a confession while one is handcuffed is no easy task. Upon completing it, Robert called for a guard, who soon peered through the window and growled, "What do you want?"

"Here's my confession," Robert replied.

"Give it to me!" the guard commanded.

After handing over his confession, Robert faced a dilemma. To stop praying was something he could not do. So pray he did, dangerous as it was. Of course, if he prayed silently, no one could read his mind, but there was always the chance that he would forget and pray as he was accustomed to by reverently bowing his head or closing his eyes. Standing in front of the window was suspicious—especially because no one was allowed to stand. Lowering his head or shutting his eyes would be too obvious. Were he to do so, everyone in the cell would know what he was doing. If his cellmates observed him praying, he didn't mind; however, he did not wish to be caught by a guard. From that point on, he was always waiting for an opportune moment to talk to God. When one came, he would seize his chance and move toward the window, but as he prayed he listened for danger.

Hearing the footfall of trouble approaching one day, he hastily returned to his seat. When the guard checked, everything looked proper. He announced through the window, "Exercise time!" The inmates arose, lined up, and began circling the room. Many took this as an opportunity to talk with each other. As Robert turned a corner, an inmate approached him and announced, "I attended a church once."

Robert considered how to answer. Had a fellow Christian noticed his witness? Was this man interested in Jesus, or did he hope to betray Robert to the guards for personal gain? Had he attended only once, or had he been a regular member? Was he a government spy or a backslidden Christian? Choosing his words carefully, Robert asked, "Which one?"

"It was built in the shape of a Bible."

Immediately recognizing the church, Robert exclaimed in amazement, "That's where I attended!" It was none other than the Seventh-day Adventist Bible Auditorium in Shanghai, which had been architecturally laid out in the shape of an open Bible.

Before they could talk any further, the guard declared, "Stop! Back in your places!"

Robert and his new friend, Mr. Lai Chi, sat in their assigned seats on opposite sides of the room. Robert longed to learn what kind of Christian his new friend was. From that time on, risky though it was, the two made excuses to communicate. At times when the guard was at the other end of the prison, Robert approached his new friend. "May I borrow some tissue?" he asked. "I'll return it to you when my family delivers some."

Without hesitation, Mr. Lai took out his roll of tissue and tore off some. Immediately, Robert sat on the toilet, which was next to his seat, and then returned to his spot on the floor.

When the next delivery of necessities arrived from his family, Robert used it as another excuse to talk with Mr. Lai. Calling for a guard, he announced that he wished to write a confession. Happily, the guard gave Robert paper and pen. "Call again when you're done," the guard said. "I'll pick them up."

When the guard's footfall sounded distant, Robert took some tissue, placed it over the paper and wrote some Bible promises on it. Folding it, he wrote out a confession for the guards and beckoned them. After the guard had taken what he wanted, Robert waited for an opportune time, and handed Lai Chi the tissue with the Bible text on it. "I'm returning the tissue I borrowed," he said loudly enough for the others to hear, then returned to his seat.

Not long afterward, Mr. Lai arose and sat on the toilet. There he unrolled the tissue, read Robert's messages, committed them to memory, wiped, and disposed of the evidence. Later Mr. Lai reversed the process, sending Robert notes on tissue.

By passing notes in this fashion, Robert learned that Lai Chi had spent six years in the detention house and that he had no relatives in

Shanghai, so no one could help him. Whenever possible, Robert shared clothes, medicines, and necessities with him.

Sometimes they talked softly together while Mr. Lai was on the toilet. Soon Robert noticed that this young man was making frequent visits and sitting an inordinate amount of time. While it gave them an opportunity to talk, Robert suspected his friend was not well. Seeing spots of red on the young man's tissue seemed to indicate a problem.

Robert was not alone in his observation. In time the guards called Mr. Lai's number and transferred him to the hospital. When he returned, he was the newcomer to the cell and was assigned the seat nearest the toilet—which just happened to be next to Robert! The new seating arrangement permitted them endless time to communicate. Speaking so softly to each other that the other inmates would have difficulty hearing, the two shared much about each other. Robert learned that Mr. Lai had suffered from a laundry list of ailments, including a bleeding ulcer, which explained the red stains on the tissue. He was a Hong Kong resident who loved to visit Shanghai without the legal travel papers. As Hongkongers could not easily obtain travel papers to enter Communist China at the time, any trip into Shanghai from Hong Kong would have been suspect. On his latest visit, he had been caught and thrown in prison.

Robert spent considerable time teaching him Christianity. It was imperative that no one, least of all the guards, realize that two Christians were sitting side by side in one cell. Were the fact discovered, the two would be separated.

Though he spent a significant amount of time teaching the Hongkonger about Jesus, Robert did not stop his routine of praying before his window of heaven. Once, while he stood at the window, an old man named Chan, whose seat was by the guard's window, stood beside Robert and announced, "I'll follow you." Obviously he knew that Robert was praying. Robert rejoiced that he had found another kindred spirit within his cell. Soon they were both silently talking to God at the window of heaven.

As they stood and prayed, Old Chan told Robert a little about his past. Gradually, bit by bit, Robert was able to piece together Old Chan's story. Terrible it was.

The Window of Heaven

The old man was a Christian university graduate. He had also been a capitalist and a member of the YMCA. Any one of those "stinking" categories was enough to get him classified as a dirty "intellectual" and place him on the government's black list. But what angered the government officials most was that Old Chan was a Christian. This had led to his arrest.

To free the old man from the greed of private enterprise, the police stuck pins into his lips, placed heavy objects around his neck, and called him a capitalist. After placing a suit and tie on him, they ridiculed him for following Western imperialism by wearing its decadent attire. Calling the suit a symbol of his wicked past, they scolded him because, by selling at a profit, he had knowingly exploited the masses for his own benefit.

Robert soon learned that the tortures Old Chan had endured for being a "capitalist pig" were mild compared to the efforts the police had made to persuade him to give up his belief in Jesus Christ. Calling him "a running dog of the imperialists" because he had accepted their God, they ordered him to get down on his hands and knees and run like a dog. As he crawled around, the officials demanded that he renounce Jesus. Soon the pressure grew too much for Old Chan. His faith faltered, and he recanted, hoping that by doing so he could live the rest of his life in peace, but he was mistaken. His sins were too great for China during the so-called Great Cultural Revolution. Despite his recantation, he was placed in prison. By the time he and Robert met, the old man had served ten years behind bars. Seeing Robert pray under the window had rekindled his interest in Christ.

Sad though the story was, Robert rejoiced that prison life had helped Old Chan accept his Savior again. Now that Robert had two inmates with whom he could talk freely, he felt God had led him into that cell. Three Christians in a cell of twelve prisoners seemed remarkable indeed. More remarkable was that they were not immediately reported. Could it be that the other prisoners were unaware? Or were they merely waiting for an opportune time? Robert took advantage of every moment to talk about Jesus with the young Hongkonger, Lai Chi, and with the older man, Old Chan. He never knew when they would be discovered and transferred.

CHAPTER 15

Two Squabbling Hypocrites

In winter, Robert and his cellmates finished supper at 4:35 P.M. and were required to sit quietly until nine before they were allowed to sleep. During those hours, the north wind sang "rhapsodies in blew" to the depressed inmates.

"Hey, criminal 153, why don't you tell us some Bible stories?" one of Robert's cellmates suggested one night.

Being given the opportunity to witness to the entire group was exciting. However, it revealed that his secret discussions with the two Christian companions—the Hongkonger, Lai Chi, and Old Chan—had not gone unnoticed. Did the request mean that Robert's inmates approved? Or did they merely want proof so that they could turn him in and gain themselves some merit?

Considering the risks quickly, Robert decided it better to obey God than man. It was his duty to share stories of the Bible whenever possible. He would sow in nights of danger as well as in days of comfort.

Beginning with the story of Creation, he explained the origin of the weekly cycle. With the story of Noah, he explained why a dove carrying an olive branch symbolizes peace. The prisoners could especially relate to the story about the wolf that dressed like a sheep. Soon Robert was telling stories practically every night, much to the enjoyment of his fellow sufferers. Their appreciation was reward enough to counter the risk.

In time, Robert discovered that two of the older men in the cell were not new to Christianity. One was a scientist named Lam Ho Yin, who had received a decadent doctoral degree from Johns Hopkins University in the United States. The other, Pang Tin, had been classified as a capitalist because he had once owned a large store in Shanghai.

Shortly before Robert had begun telling them stories in the evenings, he recalled, the former shopkeeper, Pang Tin, had tempted him by saying, "Prisoner 153, I think you're probably a doctor or an import-export trader, or—" Pausing, he had added with a knowing tone in his voice, "maybe you're a minister." Because it was against the rules for any of the prisoners to discuss their cases with fellow inmates, Robert did not know what to say. So he just smiled.

Then Pang Tin said, "My wife is a zealous Christian. She's a pianist in the church, but I must confess that during the three years of Natural Disaster,[1] cigarettes were very rare and I used pages from the Bible for my tobacco." Speaking with a broad grin, he added, "Now I realize my sin." Robert immediately recognized the hypocrisy of a smiling tiger and felt he needed to be careful around the former shopkeeper.

Robert became suspicious of Lam Ho Yin also because he openly criticized religion. Yet many had witnessed him with his hand on his breast and his eyes closed in front of the window where Robert prayed whenever he had a chance. No one in the cell could be sure where the scientist stood on the matter, but none of them would have guessed that he had been arrested on account of his religion.

As time wore on, it became evident that indeed the shopkeeper was a religious man—of sorts. The two elderly men often quarreled over religion with a younger man in the cell. After each quarrel, the aged men reported on each other to the police. Guards then escorted them down the hall to confess further.

One day, after the old men had filed reports, Pang Tin was summoned to an interview. When he returned, the guard looked in Robert's direction and shouted, "Prisoner 153, gather your stuff."

Robert obeyed. The guard led him into a smaller, empty cell and left. Alone, Robert guessed that the Pang Tin, the former shopkeeper, had betrayed him. Perhaps he had told the guards that he was telling Bible stories. Possibly he had told them that Robert was a minister. Unsure what had been the old man's motivation—fear, or a desire to gain merit—Robert was certain that he had been betrayed as a result of the shopkeeper's hypocrisy.

With nothing better to do, Robert sat on the floor and looked around. The cell was about six feet by nine. With no faces to examine, there were only bare walls and a small westward window with steel bars. Robert remembered that whenever Abraham arrived in a new place, he set up an altar and prayed. Robert did just that. "God," he prayed, "You led me to this prison within a prison. Let me see nothing save You alone." Opening his eyes, he stood and paced the cell as he sang lines from the hymn, "How Firm a Foundation."

Suddenly, a guard pushed open the panel window and railed at him, "Even now, you still sing songs."

Not wanting to talk to the guard for fear it would turn into an argument, Robert sat for a while.

Prison Instructor Chui slid the panel window open. "Give me an account of what you've said and done in the cell. Start from the time you entered this detention house."

Hearing the order, Robert initially felt like a bird in a cage. Then he remembered that his prisoner number was 153, the number for the Chinese hymn, "All the Way My Savior Leads Me." Comforted, he concluded that all he needed to report were Bible texts and common medical facts.

Grabbing the opportunity, he took pen in hand and began to write his first true confession. It was a perfect opportunity to witness to the guards and to his prison instructors, whose job it was to reprogram him to fit into New China by giving up his superstitious ideas about a man from Bethlehem who had died and was said to have been resurrected and returned to heaven. He wrote, "I told my fellow inmates about the beginning of the era, the origin of the weekly cycle, and the history of the red dress.[2] I explained why a dove carrying a new leaf in its beak symbolizes peace. I also recited the story of the ferocious wolf in sheep's clothing. And I showed them that important communist principles have everything in common with Christianity. For instance, the roots of communist teachings such as 'give to everyone as he needs' and 'if a man does not work, he should not eat,' came originally from the Bible." Having completed his confession, Robert called for the guard, who dutifully took it and left.

Prison Instructor Chui never asked Robert for another confession. They gave him no obvious response, either positive or negative. As time passed, Robert decided to leave the matter with God.

One day, when his can of food was passed in, Robert found diced pork mixed into his rice. Prisoners were served pork once or twice a week. On those days, because he had told the guards he did not eat pork for religious reasons, they had served him egg instead.

Now he was being served pork again. Thinking it must have been a mistake, he immediately called for a guard.

When the guard arrived, Robert reported, "There's pork in my rice. Never have I eaten pork. When I came to this detention house, I explained my beliefs. Since then, you've always been kind enough to serve me the *halal*[3] food of the Muslims. May I have *halal* food again today?"

The guard sneered, "You're not a Muslim!" and closed the panel roughly.

Pork kept appearing in his food whenever the prisoners were served it. Robert did not eat. As he returned the food, he suggested, "When the others are served pork, just give me some salted vegetables."

"You're not a Muslim!" the guard shouted again. "Christians eat pork." He slammed the panel.

Robert left his food on the dish again. When the guard returned, he handed the food back, saying, "When I first came here, I explained to you that Seventh-day Adventists don't eat unclean meat. You agreed to serve me as you do the Muslims. Please, don't serve me pork. Instead, give me an egg as you used to. You can serve me *halal*, or, at least, give me salted vegetables."

In a condescending tone, the guard replied, "If you wish to get out of this prison alive, take my advice. Eat pork!"

Robert refused, and his stomach grumbled. Try as he might to persuade the guards, he felt he might as well have been conversing with the wooden floor. The guards did not listen. Robert soon realized that they were using food to break his relationship with God.

A coughing spell racked Robert's lungs. Fearing that his tuberculosis was returning, Robert's faith in God weakened. His desire to witness for God overshadowed his determination to follow God's clear instruction about diet. Ever since he had become a Seventh-day Adventist Christian, Robert had not eaten unclean meat. He stayed away from seafood. However, the thought of coughing up blood caused him to worry about his health. Forgetting the great power of God, Robert thought, *Surely God wants me to remain healthy. If I died in prison, how could I witness to the other prisoners? They might lose their faith if I were not alive to strengthen them.* On and on he struggled mentally, momentarily forgetting that Daniel and his friends remained faithful even on the matter of diet, to say nothing of Daniel's friends preferring to die in a burning fiery furnace rather than to worship the statue that Nebuchadnezzar had set up.

The next time his meal was served with pork in it, instead of trusting God to deliver him, he let his hunger and his fear of tuberculosis overpower his faith and better judgment. He ate what was served. He decided that, when he got out of solitary confinement, he could always ask for *halal* food again.

As he chewed on the diced pork, his taste buds reminded him how much he had once liked pig flesh. As the days passed, he ate whatever was served. Slowly, his strength returned and his coughing subsided.

For 110 days Robert was kept in solitary confinement in that tiny cell. It was winter, and the temperature fell as low as twenty degrees Fahrenheit for a week. Robert's towel froze. Somehow he managed to use the frozen towel to rub down his body with a few drops of water every morning.

To pass the time, Robert memorized English words alphabetically. It exercised his mind and helped him to maintain interest in living. Soon alphabetizing English became a hobby. Later Robert grew tired of the game, but not before God used it to teach him a valuable lesson. Having recalled all the words he could think of that began with the letter "J," it suddenly dawned on him that he had forgotten the words "Jehovah" and "Jesus." He chided himself for not thinking of them sooner. Constantly gaining spiritual insights from his own experience, he realized that Jehovah never forgets man, but it is easy for man to forget Jehovah. "Forget *me* not" is human nature. But if one forgets self, one is happier. It was a message Robert felt he needed at the time.

When Robert wanted to take a break from his English word game, he composed poems mentally. Having no pen or paper, he could not record them. It worked out to his advantage. Written down, they could have fallen into the wrong hands.

When Christmas arrived, Robert couldn't see the snow, but he had a white Christmas just the same. The light outside reflected off the snow extraordinarily brightly on the wall. Alone though he was in his cell, Robert felt the presence of Jesus, his beloved Savior. He recalled that Jesus, the King of the Universe, had once been a helpless babe in Bethlehem. As he looked around at his own humble surroundings, he reminded himself that Jesus had been born beside animals in a lowly, smelly stable.

Robert sang a Christmas hymn that he had composed many years earlier. He had written it on a Christmas Eve, when he was inspired by a pastor arrested for his faith and forced to leave his family. He had many children, one of whom had been born only days before the arrest. Robert had sent the poem to the pastor hidden in a box of candy. It asked what kind of sacrifice Jesus suffered for humanity. A dark night, a dirty manger, a chilly wind surrounded Him on his first night on earth.

After singing the hymn, Robert thought to himself, *Now, I myself am in prison, as the pastor was. Let me meditate on our Lord's love. Let me, who am like a bird shut in a cage under a black cloth, learn the songs my Master would teach me.*

Hymns and songs became Robert's good friends. He enjoyed humming Dvorak's *New World* symphony or Beethoven's Fifth Symphony. He also liked Stephen Foster's "Old Folks at Home." Sometimes, as Robert sang, tears ran down his cheeks.

Alone in the little cell, Robert celebrated his thirtieth birthday. That day he thought about Jesus at age thirty. Jesus had left His home and His mother to march on the blood-stained way. The cross called Him from afar. Robert, too, had been called to take up his cross and follow Him. How glorious it was, Robert thought, that his Savior had led him to suffer for Him in this little cell.

PRISONER FOR CHRIST

One day Robert heard the guards singing Mao's songs outside. It was 1966, the beginning of the Great Cultural Revolution. At the middle school across the street from the Number One Detention Center, students from the high school had poured onto the street singing Mao's songs. At that moment, Robert seemed to receive a vision that at some time in the future many of God's people would be anointed with the Holy Spirit. With zealous hearts, they would take the Bible and go from one place to another, crossing rivers and climbing mountains to sow the seed of the Gospel.

Robert remembered that many years earlier he had had a very simple dream that there would be light in every home in China—even in the countryside. This dream has since been fulfilled literally with the coming of electricity to China, but Robert took his dream to have a spiritual meaning. As the Bible promises, "The people who sat in darkness have seen a great Light, and for those who sat in the region and shadow of death, Light has dawned" (Matthew 4:16). Robert thought such a day must come and could not be delayed much longer. Inspired by his vision that had reminded him of his earlier dream, Robert felt a fire burning in his lonely heart on that severe winter night.

Just before Chinese New Year, 110 days after Robert had been placed in solitary confinement, guards escorted him back to his former cell. When the door opened and the cellmates saw him, they were stunned. As nobody knew when they might be called for execution, his cellmates had not expected to see him again. The one most stunned was Pang Tin, the old man who had accused Robert before Prison Instructor Chui. He looked decidedly embarrassed.

Soon Robert was again discussing the Bible with his faithful Christian friends, Lai Chi and Old Chan. Well aware that Pang Tin, the old shopkeeper, could report them, they worried that they would be separated again.

On January 15, about one month after Robert's return to his old cell, everything changed. The guards slid open the panel window and declared, "Pack up, criminals! Straighten up your stuff and wait for further information!"

What would happen next? Robert wondered. Had one of the squabbling hypocrites reported? Robert feared for his two Christian companions. What would their future be if they were isolated? Would they give up their faith? Or would they remain strong?

Robert and the Hongkonger exchanged glances. Almost simultaneously, their eyes met with those of Old Chan. From the look in the others' eyes, it appeared as though they all shared the same dread of separation. As Robert packed, he figured it would be the last time he would ever see these Christian companions.

---

[1] 1958-1962. During this time, China experienced widespread crop failure, which resulted in famine. In the worst-hit provinces, the government even allowed people to beg for food.

[2] Prostitutes wear red in China as they did in Bible times and still do in the Middle East. Women who wear red in these countries are considered for hire sexually. Robert used this as a springboard to talk about the whore of Revelation.

[3] *Halal* meat, like kosher meat, comes from an animal drained of blood following the tradition of Islam for *halal* and Judaism for kosher meat; also, no pork is served, because both Islam and Judaism forbid it to be eaten.

CHAPTER 16

The Red Guard

Not having been told why they were being transferred made Robert's cellmates nervous. Some of them feared they had been selected for execution. They struggled with the guards, who relentlessly pushed them down the halls and out the doors. There, for the first time, they met with youthful guards wearing red arm bands. Robert surmised they must be the Red Guards they had read about in the local newspaper, the *Liberation Daily*. Their violent deeds were repeatedly glorified in the press. School-age youth, they, with the government's blessing, disregarded Confucius' age-old teaching of respect for teachers, elders, and superiors. Touting the Little Red Book of Chairman Mao's quotations, the Red Guards proudly broke up families, taunted elders, and placed dunce caps upon their teachers' heads before parading them through the streets as fools. Robert noticed they were holding whips.

About three hundred prisoners from other cells joined Robert's group. Under the watchful eye of rifle-toting soldiers from the People's Liberation Army, cruel Red Guard youth whipped any reluctant prisoner into line as they began packing the inmates into several large red garrison trucks. Soon many of the prisoners decided boarding the vehicles would bring relief from the Red Guards' fury.

One inmate became so scared when he was lashed by a whip that he began singing the Communist Party anthem. Robert guessed that the man had once been a member of the Party and had fallen from grace. In his piteous state, the man undoubtedly hoped to curry favor by revealing his loyalty.

The song earned him no merit. Singling him out, a Red Guard shouted, "Who do you think you are, singing that song? Did you forget what you are? You're a criminal or you wouldn't be standing here! You're unfit to sing this song." Grabbing him, the youth pulled him out of line and beat him mercilessly.

Several asked where they were being taken. "To an unknown location," the guards barked. As far as the prisoners were concerned, that dreadful answer was worse than no reply at all. When all were in with the doors shut, it was dark inside. Then the locks clicked.

The ride was tense for the crowded inmates. So real was their fear that Robert felt he could touch it. With the Cultural Revolution in full force, death could strike at any moment.

As the vehicle made left and right turns on its way down the road, a ten-year veteran of the prison announced, "We're not going to be executed. Maybe we're being transferred to another detention center because our prison was too full." Some apparently believed him, while others doubted.

Squatting as best he could, Robert prayed silently. As the vehicle tossed and turned, he thought, *My life belongs to the Lord. As Paul once said, "I am the Lord's prisoner."* Then he prayed again. *O Lord, let me see Your controlling hand in a wheel intersecting a wheel. Lord, you showed Elijah the earthquake, the fire, and the wind, but You were not there. Instead You were in the still small voice. Please, let me hear Your tender whisper now. Let me be inside Your ark as the raging waves surround it.*

Suddenly the driver stopped and the guards jumped down and shouted orders. When the door of the vehicle was unlocked, the criminals spilled out. One prisoner, certain that he was about to be executed, began singing "Le Internationale." Angered by the man's "bourgeois" song, the youthful Red Guards scourged him severely.

Once Robert's feet were on firm ground, he looked up at the stars for the first time in more than two years. The sky was clear with no obstacles in the way. A sickle-shaped moon shone brightly. Spotting several of the constellations instantly, he searched for Orion. Gazing into the heavens reminded him of the majesty of His God and man's smallness. Yet, insignificant though he was compared to the vast universe, God cared about him. With his soul nourished, he praised God. Words from the second chapter of Daniel came to his mind. Despite what the Communists claimed, everything around him was temporary. Someday, as the interpretation of Nebuchadnezzar's dream revealed, an Unhewn Stone would deliver him from this cruel world. The thought comforted him.

"There will be three criminals to a cell." A guard's voice interrupted Robert's peaceful moment. "Criminals' numbers will be called at random, so don't expect to see a familiar face!" The guards began calling numbers. Groups of three were escorted into the Number Two Detention Center. Soon Robert heard his number. To his surprise and joy, the numbers of his two Christian friends were called immediately afterward. That meant they would share the same cell. Given the number of prisoners, the odds were impossible. It had to be a miracle, Robert thought.

After guards led the three Christians down a hall, they found themselves locked into a seven-by-nine-foot cell. One wall was made of bars from ceiling to floor, giving the prisoners a view of the center of the building. While the bars made the environment more stimulating than it had been in the cells of the previous prison, they also made it easier for the guards to watch the prisoners. Yet, happily, it meant that Robert could keep an eye on the guards too.

Then there was the noise factor. As inmates in surrounding cells read from Chairman Mao's book or sang political songs, communication between Robert and his friends became a challenge. However, the noise also made it difficult for the guards to eavesdrop.

Robert sat observing the guards and learned that, as they made their rounds, they could only watch certain sections. It became evident that it was impossible for them to watch the entire prison all the time. This enabled the three Christians to exploit their advantages.

Robert suggested a clever, though subtly deceptive plan. They would keep Mao's Little Red Book in hand while he talked about the Bible and led them in song. The others immediately approved. As they talked and sang together, they listened for the footfall of the guard or looked for his shadow. When they sensed the coming of a guard or saw the shadow, they immediately began reading the words of Chairman Mao. As soon as the guard was beyond earshot, they returned to discussing Bible topics and singing hymns. Then Robert began putting verses from the Bible into song. His friends eagerly sang with him. Soon they had committed the verses to memory.

Old Chan was called frequently for questioning, while Robert and the Hongkonger, Lai Chi, were usually ignored. Upon returning from an inquisition one day, Old Chan hinted that he might be leaving soon. Robert wondered about the old man's future. Not long afterward, a guard showed up, called Old Chan's prison number and ordered, "Pack up!"

The old man obeyed.

Robert and Lai Chi watched as the guard escorted him down the hall. For some time after that, the two shared the room alone, which afforded them time for intense religious study.

Confident in each other's loyalty, the Hongkonger talked to Robert about himself. "I was once a Seventh-day Adventist in Hong Kong, but after my travels to Shanghai, I gave up my religion."

"I thought you were a Christian when we met," Robert said.

"After my arrest," Lai Chi replied, "I shared a cell with a Catholic priest. Once, when all the inmates from my cell were showering in the prison shower room, the priest seized the opportunity to ask if I wanted to be baptized. When I consented, he cupped his hands in the shower, captured some water, and poured it over my head."

Robert smiled when he heard the evidence that Christians were being baptized in prison by the very inmates who had been arrested for proselytizing. Feeling strongly that God had arranged their meeting, Robert said, "Now you've come full circle."

"I don't understand," was the Hongkonger's response. "What circle?"

"You were a Seventh-day Adventist in Hong Kong, and after rejecting your faith, you subsequently accepted Catholicism. You have now met me and returned to believing Adventism's literal interpretation of the Bible." Lai Chi nodded that he understood.

One morning an unusual aroma filled the cells. "They're cooking fish," Lai Chi announced.

Sure enough, the guards served fish. When Robert saw his meal, he had to admit to himself that the fish looked better than the regular menu. Ever since Robert, while serving time in solitary confinement, began eating pork, the guards continued to give him the same food that the other inmates ate. Having once yielded to temptation regarding diet, Robert was too afraid to ask for *halal* food or steamed vegetables again.

While the prisoners were noisily enjoying the special treat, the guards distributed the local newspaper, the *Liberation Daily*. Picking up his copy, Robert began reading it to Lai Chi. The front-page story was about the 1967 war[1] in the Middle East. The *Liberation Daily* thought Israel's fight with its Arab neighbors might lead to a terrible world war with no winners.

"Do you think this war is a sign that Jesus is coming soon?" the Hongkonger asked.

"I don't know," Robert replied thoughtfully. "But I do know that if Jesus comes, my days in this prison will soon be over!"

So significant was the news to Robert that, when the guards retrieved the aluminum boxes that contained his food, he failed to notice that he had eaten nothing.

Shortly after the Six-Day War, the guards placed a third prisoner in Robert's cell called Old Leung. The newcomer was an elderly man whose teeth were badly damaged. His glasses, like his spirit, were broken. He sat in his corner and often sighed dejectedly. Neither Robert nor Lai Chi knew anything about him. Once Robert felt certain that the newcomer had fallen asleep the night of his arrival, Robert suggested to the Hongkonger, "Why don't we discontinue our religious conversations until we know more about our new cellmate?"

Lai Chi concurred. "Let's be sure he's no Judas."

---

[1] This conflict later became known as the Six Day War, a short-lived but earth-shaking conflict. In six literal days Israel destroyed the armies of Egypt, Jordan, Syria, and Iraq in blitzkrieg attacks that shocked the Arab world and amazed the West. China and Russia supported the Palestinians. The Palestinian Liberation Organization (PLO) has long had an embassy in Beijing. At the time, many Christians, including some Adventist leaders and writers, wondered whether the 1967 war was a fulfillment of Old Testament prophecy.

CHAPTER 17

The Storm

T empting the newcomer to reveal his identity and case history was no easy task, because prisoners were forbidden to discuss these topics. Nevertheless, from time to time, Robert posed probing questions that he hoped, if answered, would reveal more about the newcomer than about himself. When Robert learned that the newcomer, Old Leung, was a journalist, he feared him. A journalist's job was to report! It seemed to Robert that, as long as Old Leung was in the room, Robert would be unable to teach the Bible to the Lai Chi. Yet he determined to discover whether the journalist could be trusted.

Continuing his probing questions, Robert asked one day, "Why do you sigh?"

"*Wo mae ban fa!*" wailed Old Leung. "My case is impossible. There's no way out of this mess. Both the Kuomintang and the Communists hate me."

"How do you know?" Robert inquired.

"Oh, they have their reasons. Back when Chairman Mao and his followers were outlaws living in caves, I gave money to support their movement. Then there was the time I helped some Communists escape from China. Now that the Great Helmsman's in power, thanks in part to me, prison is my reward. I've been used and discarded. I should be a founding Party member. Oh, it's not fair!" He sighed loudly.

"Why would they be angry with you?" Robert probed.

"They're upset with me because, whenever President Chiang Kai-shek's forces, the ruling Kuomintang, did something right, I praised them in my articles. I was just being honest and fair to both sides. That was my job! I was honest and fair with them, but they have not returned the favor." He sighed again. "It's not fair! Today, even though the Communists hate me, the Kuomintang wants nothing to do with me. None of them will help me escape across the Taiwan Strait to freedom, because I once supported the Communists before the Kuomintang fled in defeat to Taiwan. My heart is heavily weighted. That's why you hear me frequently sighing."

Once Robert understood that the journalist had enemies in both camps, he grew bolder in his approach. At an appropriate moment, he said, "As a journalist, you must be familiar with the writings of many great authors. Who do you think wrote the greatest literature of all time?"

Instantly the journalist replied, "Tolstoy and Twain."

"I'm familiar with both of them," Robert replied.

Seemingly impressed, Old Leung asked, "What do you think is the greatest literature ever written?"

"The Bible." Robert wondered what the journalist would do with the bait. He could get Robert in trouble by reporting to the guards that Robert had placed the Bible on a higher level than Chairman Mao's writings, but then Old Leung had already incriminated himself by placing Tolstoy and Twain above Mao. Robert had carefully couched his view of the Bible's greatness from a cultural and not from a religious standpoint.

"The Bible is not literature!" the journalist retorted.

"Did you know that many great writers quoted the Bible in their masterpieces?"

Old Leung admitted he was unaware.

"Tolstoy read the Bible, and Twain quoted it. Some of Twain's best allusions were derived from the Bible. The Bible is a great book of literature."

They changed the subject, and Robert waited to see if the journalist would file a report. He did not have long to wait before guards came and took Old Leung down the hall to be interviewed. As he left,

The Storm

Robert and the Hongkonger exchanged nervous glances. What would happen when the guards returned?

Nothing happened.

Robert grew bolder. One day his relatives sent him some Rainbow brand soap. On the bar was imprinted a rainbow. Turning to the journalist, he asked, "Do you know the story of the rainbow?"

When Old Leung allowed that he didn't, Robert told the story of Noah and the flood. "According to the Bible," he concluded, "the rainbow is God's sign that He promises never to destroy the earth with a worldwide flood again." The pounding of Robert's heart told him he feared he might have overstepped his bounds. Would the journalist callously betray him in a desperate attempt to gain some degree of merit?

Soon after Robert had told the story of Noah, Old Leung banged on the bars, calling for a guard. "Paper!" he demanded when the guard arrived. Paper and pen were supplied. The journalist wrote fast and furiously, finished, and shouted again until he attracted a guard's attention. Not long after he had filed the confession, he was summoned down the hall again.

Robert suspected the worst.

Guards escorted Old Leung back to the cell a few hours later. As they opened the cell door to let him in, Robert feared that he would be called next, but the guards left without a word. Guessing that the journalist had said nothing about the story of Noah, Robert waited for another opportunity to test him. At yuletide, he dared to share with him the biblical story of Christmas. When no one came and separated the two Christians, Robert decided Old Leung could be trusted. He and Lai Chi renewed their Bible discussions. Soon the journalist joined in.

One night, a terrible storm struck Shanghai. Water poured from the roof and sprayed from the commons area into the prison cells. Trapped, the inmates worried that they might drown. To avoid being drenched, Robert and his cellmates moved to the back of their cell.

What did such a terrible storm mean? Was it a sign? Thinking about the life of Paul, Robert wondered, *Did God send the storm to free me from prison? Or was it a shipwreck? Am I to die in prison or be deliv-*

ered from my captors? In either case, he concluded, Paul took advantage of the situation to witness for Christ.

The pounding of the rain against the roof was deafening. Robert sensed his cellmates' fear. As a pastor, he had to think of some way to help them. But what? His words were drowned by the storm. Shouting as best he could, he suggested that they hold hands and sing.

They sang hymns and held hands until the storm, and their fears, subsided. It was truly a night to remember.

****

One day the guards made two announcements that altered prison life for the better. The first was that visitations would be allowed. Robert's heart leaped for joy at the news. At long last he could see his family again after four years of separation.

Hearing the guard's voice demanding attention again, Robert listened. "Prisoners can write letters to their families—provided they follow prison regulations," the guard shouted. "The letters will be approved by a guard to make sure their tone is upbeat and that they do not exceed one hundred Chinese characters. Send letters to your family inviting them to visit you!"

Robert could hardly contain his excitement. He had been begging the guards to let him see his mother or sister, but the guards had repeatedly denied his request unless he confessed his crimes. Believing himself innocent, he had not cooperated and had foregone family visitations. His heart raced at the thought that he might see his loved ones soon.

In the night, lying on the floor by the prison bars, his thoughts returned to Mary. He badly wanted to share the rest of his life with her, but, he reminded himself, she was not getting any younger. If, God forbid, he did not live to be released, she might miss her chance to find a husband. Perhaps it would be better if he told her not to wait.

His thoughts drifted to what he should tell his relatives when they came. What would he say about Mary? Should he tell her to find someone else? Perhaps he should write it in a letter, he thought. No, the guards would read it. They would learn that she was his weak point and use her to try to destroy him. He decided that he should bring it up during a visitation. When would his number be called?

He lay for a while, looking at the ceiling, letting his thoughts wander.

If his family could visit him, he thought, perhaps they could bring him gifts. Chinese traditionally bring gifts whenever they visit someone. Naturally, his family would want to know if he needed anything. What did he need? Not much. He had so little space in his tiny cell. Besides, they were already sending him toilet paper, medicine, and other daily supplies. Deep down, he knew there was something he wanted badly—a Bible. How could he get one? He couldn't just ask for one in a letter. The guard would never approve such a request. Prisoners could read only Chairman Mao's Little Red Book of quotations. Bibles were strictly forbidden. They were banned not just in prison but throughout China. If he asked for one, what kind of trouble might his family get into? He would have to ask for a Bible in code. But how?

CHAPTER 18

Sentenced Without Trial

Sitting on the floor—he could hardly remember what sitting on a chair was like—Robert pushed a needle and thread through his rags. He didn't have anything particular to mend, but the weekly activity gave him something to kill the boredom. It was Sunday, August 25, 1968, another day Robert would long remember. It was just under four years after the day he had been arrested and placed in detention awaiting trial. He and the others were just finishing their "Sunday sewing" when they heard the guards approaching to pick up the needles. After handing them over, the cellmates straightened the room and awaited the last meal of the "busy Sunday."

To Robert's surprise, the guard on duty, whom the prisoners had nicknamed "Bluster," shouted Robert's new ID number, "Prisoner 468!" he shouted. "You're dishonest! You must give an account for all your crimes. Come out right now."

Fear filled the cell, but then Robert winked at his two cellmates. In seconds all three were winking at each other. They knew that, since none of them had violated any prison rules other than talking about the Bible, their case was as clear as a new day dawning. The only question was: Had someone in the next room overheard and betrayed them?

Shanghai summers are scorching hot, and the heat wave that year had extended into the fall. As Robert was wearing only shorts, he quickly pulled on a sweatshirt and slipped into his sandals. He had no time to dress further, for the guard had unlocked the door and ordered him to follow.

Down the hall to the corner of the stairway they went. Then the guard said, "Stop here!"

Robert stopped.

Another officer stood nearby, apparently awaiting Robert's arrival. When their eyes met, Robert immediately recognized the officer. He was the prison accountant.

"You listen carefully," the accountant began. "I now represent the Shanghai Public Security Organization, the Procuratorial Organization, and the People's Courts." While he rattled off all his titles, trying to make himself sound important because he had gained so many positions, Robert reminded himself that the three positions had recently been united and placed under the control of the military. In actual fact, though he held many titles, the accountant held only one position. "I am here to give you your sentence," the accountant announced. Pulling a sheet of paper from his pocket, he read, "Robert Huang: Counterrevolutionary. Criminal Huang is a transgressor. His ideas are antiParty. He needs to be reformed to fit into New China. . . ."

Robert heard no more because he was amazed that he had been denied a trial. His sentence was being read to him in the hallway of the Number Two Detention Center. While he had languished in his cell, he had long anticipated the day when his case would come to trial, where he might be able to prove his innocence. Or at least those who were in attendance could determine whether his sentence was just. He had hoped to be like Paul and have an opportunity to share his faith with a magistrate. But, as he heard his sentence read, he knew it was not to be. There was nothing public or open about it. Perhaps, he thought, they had been unable to discover any crime they could sustain in court. While he felt cheated out of his trial, he also felt somewhat relieved, especially when, at the end of the paper, he heard the guard say, "Criminal Huang is sentenced to four years in Number Three Detention Center." At long last he was no longer a prisoner awaiting sentence. He comforted himself with the thought that the floor would not rot beneath him before he got out.

Being sentenced truly gave him comfort. After serving four years without knowing how long he would remain in a cell before his case could be reviewed for sentencing, he could now be certain that, eventually, he would be released. His relief was not without trepidation. He dreaded the thought of serving time in Number Three Detention Center. His soon-to-be new home was a gigantic jail with ten five-story buildings. In his boyhood, he had often walked passed the Number Three Detention Center. Every time he had done so, he had averted his eyes. What went on behind its walls had always been shrouded in mystery. Never had he dreamed that someday he, too, would serve time behind the foreboding walls. How would he survive sharing tight quarters with convicted rapists, thieves, and murderers?

After taking Robert back to his cell, the guard ordered, "Pack up!"

Hurriedly gathering his meager belongings, Robert had little time for goodbyes. All too soon, the guard reappeared, unlocked the door and led Robert outside to a blue truck loaded with other prisoners destined to serve time in the Number Three Detention Center. The ride to their new home was short, but as they passed through the streets, many pedestrians noticed the criminals and jeered, while others looked away in disgust or fear. The day was hotter than usual. While Robert and the others were being shown their new quarters, water rations were being distributed throughout the center. The floor, flooded from prisoners bathing, scrubbing, cleaning, and brushing during the distribution, was slippery.

"*Quai diar! Quai diar!*" shouted the guards as they marched through the lobby and down the hall toward the cells. "Hurry up, criminals! Faster!"

Sweating profusely, Robert and the other newcomers had no choice but to carry their heavy bags and, without slipping on the wet floor, try to keep up with the guards. Robert saw many faces pressed close to the iron bars and felt many curious eyes following his every step. Apparently, their arrival was uncommon entertainment. Elsewhere, he heard sighs, groans, and mournful songs.

Eventually they stopped on the second floor. Three prisoners were locked into a seven-foot-by-nine-foot cell. Robert thought he could never really get used to the cramped living quarters but reminded himself that he had grown somewhat accustomed to cramped living over the last four years. When he settled in, it was nearly supper time. While waiting for the mess tins to be served, Robert and his cellmates quietly shared their impressions of their new home. Robert suggested, "The ten buildings are like the hills of Rome."

A cellmate pointed out that the shape of the building was quite similar to that of the Number Two Detention Center.

"This one has one more floor than the other," said the third. "Each floor has ninety-six cells. With three prisoners in each cell, that means we share the floor with 287 fellow inmates."

The tins of tasteless food arrived. Everyone ate as if it were delicious, which indeed it was to stomachs that were near starvation. After the empty tins had been picked up, the next thing the inmates knew, the guards had rung the bell, signaling time to sleep. Attempting to show his Christian spirit, Robert volunteered to sleep beside the wooden commode, protecting his cellmates from being dripped on. As he lay beside the commode, the dim light in the cell intensified the gloom.

The next morning, Robert discovered through casual conversation that his cellmates were both criminal offenders. One was old; the other young. One was serving a three-year sentence and the other seven years. "If I combine my four-year detention awaiting sentence with my four-year sentence," Robert said softly, "I'll be serving the longest time. In fact, I'll still be in this cell after both of you are released." The others smiled broadly. The time Robert was required to serve behind bars coincided with the government's attitude that counterrevolutionaries were more to be feared than criminal offenders.

The older criminal, Old Huang, whose family name was identical to Robert's, had a fierce-looking face. He had committed adultery, which was a crime in New China. He was illiterate and asked, "Could you write a letter for me?"

"What would you like me to write?" Robert asked.

"I want my friend to repay my debt." At first Robert thought it was a waste of time to write the letter because he doubted the friend would pay, but when he learned the debt was only the cost of half a rooster, he thought the exercise absurd and hopeless. Yet it revealed that underneath the fierce exterior, his cellmate had a good heart. Even though he feared that the letter would never pass the guard's approval, he decided it wise to get along with his cellmates. In light of the tightness of the living quarters, building a good relationship was far better than fostering an air of misunderstanding. Reluctantly, thinking the guards would surely reject the letter, he acceded to the request.

Robert's other inmate, Ho Shan, was a young man with a muscular body that revealed itself whenever he pressed close to the cell's black iron bars. As he held the bars with two hands, Robert thought he appeared to be just like a wild ox. A product of the Cultural Revolution, Ho Shan became an outlaw. Once he had been a middle school student, then he had become a trainee in a factory before he had entered a life of crime. He had engaged in gang fights, beatings, vandalism, and looting. Besides that, from overhearing the young man's stories and looking at his physique, Robert concluded that he was a regular Don Juan.

Thinking about his cellmates, Robert wondered how he would be able to get along with them. Their whole experience, range of interests, and conversation were vastly different from his. Then he reminded himself that Jesus, while growing up in Nazareth, had been tempted in every way yet was without sin. Surely, in his tiny cell, he was living in a modern Nazareth. Yet Jesus had left him an inspiring example that he wanted to follow. He did not want to be haughty, but neither did he want to join in their vulgarity and evil ways. He knew he would have to be brave but cautious. It would never do for him to be a solitary flower in love with its own fragrance. He preferred to be a lotus blossom emerging unstained from the filth. Robert soon learned his goal of blooming untainted would be more of a challenge than he had first imagined. His prison was less of a reformatory and more of a huge vat of dye. If a prisoner did not set high standards and conduct himself well, he became stained and his character deteriorated.

Whenever he had a chance, Robert tried to lift his thoughts above his prison walls. An opportunity arose when the guard in charge of work routine posted the newcomers' ID numbers. As Robert had just arrived in the new detention house, he was considered a newcomer and issued a new prison number—1068. To his surprise, he discovered the last two numbers of his new ID were "68." Those numbers proved meaningful to him. In 1968 he had received his sentence. The hymn, "Jesus' Love Is Greater Than a Mother's Love" is number 68 in the Chinese hymnal. As he meditated further, he recalled God's promise to prisoners found in Psalm 68:6: "God bringeth out those which are bound with chains." Indeed, he smiled to himself, his prison days would pass!

As a witnessing tool, Robert did not hide his devotions. When food was served, he made it his habit to bow his head, close his eyes, and say grace before eating. In time, this aroused his cellmates' curiosity. They asked, "Why do you do that?" Immediately, Robert explained, "I'm thanking God for my food."

That evening, Ho Shan said, "Criminal Huang, I'd like to hear more about your beliefs."

Robert began by telling him the meaning of the number sixty-eight.

"How can you be so sure you're going to be released?" he asked.

Robert told him he knew God's promises were true. "I've been imprisoned only because I'm a Christian. I have committed no crime, so I have the hope that God will release me from my present bondage."

"If your God is so powerful, why did He let you be arrested?" Ho Shan asked.

"God can turn evil into good." Robert smiled. "Perhaps He wanted me to meet you here." Then he related the story of Joseph to show that the evil plans of Joseph's brothers were overturned by God. When Joseph rose to become the second-highest ruler in Egypt, he was able to save his family from famine. Then he told him about the wicked King Manasseh, whom God allowed to be arrested and thrown into a dungeon as punishment for his evil deeds. "While in prison, he prayed for deliverance, promising to worship God the rest of his life if his prayer were answered."

"What happened to the king?" Ho Shan wanted to know.

"God heard Manasseh and returned him to his throne in Israel. The king was as good as his word. God let Manasseh's enemies imprison him to give him time to examine his life and repent of his evil ways." Looking straight into the young man's eyes, Robert added, "It can be the same with you."

"Can you teach me to pray?" asked Ho Shan. Robert wrote out the Lord's Prayer for him.

A guard appeared at Robert's cell a few days later and called to Ho Shan, "You're being transferred to Number Two Detention Center." Packing quickly, the young man followed the guard.

The two remaining inmates had little time to enjoy their extra space before the guards brought a new cellmate. Like Ho Shan, the new inmate, named Wang Yan Tung, was young and was a student who had worked in a factory. When Robert introduced himself, the young man replied, "I've heard about you. I roomed with one of your cellmates. He told me about you." Soon they became well acquainted.

Wang Yan Tung told Robert that he had been incarcerated because he couldn't stand the mistreatment he had received from his stepmother. "So I planned to kill her by an electric shock and, after I was certain I had been successful, commit suicide. Meticulously, I laid out my plan. The plot would have succeeded but for an inexplicable broken circuit. My stepmother woke up and reported me to the authorities, who arrested me and gave me a seven-year sentence for attempted murder."

Robert admitted that he couldn't agree with the young man's conduct but sympathized with his situation. After explaining his point of view, Robert said, "I believe God's mercy and intervention prevented two lives from being snuffed out that day. Surely, if your plan had succeeded, you would've died with no hope of salvation."

Wang Yan Tung agreed. "I'm glad the plot failed."

They lived together one week. Then Wang Yan Tung was chosen to be a worker in the prison, and Robert was transferred to another cell.

There Robert met two counterrevolutionaries. One old man, Old Chong, was an old rich farmer. During Chairman Mao's term in office, Mao bolstered his position by creating a personality cult. Many throughout the country, including Old Chong, paraded in support of the Chairman, each holding an official Mao portrait. Suddenly it had started raining and, unconsciously, the old farmer had covered his head with the portrait. Someone saw the act and either reported it or denounced him, or both. In any case, he was arrested and given a three-year sentence. Whenever Robert tried to engage him in conversation, he only wanted to talk about his pigs and piglets! He was not concerned about politics or religion. No counterrevolutionary was he!

Robert's other cellmate, Yu Kwok, had once been the principal of an elementary school. He listened eagerly to Robert's Bible stories. Telling Bible stories, recalling Bible verses he had earlier committed to memory, or sharing his poetry and songs were all illegal activities; however, they helped to dispel a prison routine heavily overshadowed with a mounting sense of gloom.

CHAPTER 19

There's Something About Mary

Gloomy though it was in the Number Three Detention Center, the cellmates enjoyed a better life than other inmates at other prisons in some ways. Noteworthy was a monthly allowance of two renminbi. With that money, prisoners could ask the guard for toilet paper, toothpaste, pens, and some sweet Chinese medicines. Toilet paper cost around twenty fen[1] and the toothpaste about the same price.

The food was slightly better and was served twice daily. Breakfast was yam. At first the inmates enjoyed it immensely because it was sweet, but after eating it daily, they tired of it. The evening meal was rice. With it came a topping of meat or vegetable. Robert requested and once again received *halal* food. After his solitary confinement, it had taken time for him to persuade them he was serious about not eating pork. He was glad that the guards had relented. Now, whenever pork was served, the guards gave him egg instead.

Even though the food tasted better, the improvement was only incremental. It was still bland. Some prisoners flavored it by squeezing toothpaste into it. The toothpaste sweetened the rice, making it more palatable. Others requested salt and poured spoonful after spoonful into the rice. Understandably, they became thirsty and begged the guards for water. But the guards were under orders to ration the water. Only on hot days did some of the guards triple the ration, but no exceptions were made for prisoners who salted their food. Instead they scolded and mocked the thirsty prisoners, saying, "You're only waste machines. The only reason why the state keeps you alive is because you create human waste for fertilizer! Since you're of such little value, don't expect better food. You salted it yourselves; it's your own fault that you're thirsty!"

In time, the allowance and the improved menu, used unwisely, became a curse that added to the gloom. That gloominess within the cells was highly contagious. Everyone—including Robert—caught its spirit, and it seemed to hang on like a bad cold.

Shining brightly through the gloom that Robert felt within the walls was one bright spot. He could be with his family again! For Robert, it would be the first time in four years that he had been allowed to see them. The other prisoners were equally excited about the monthly visit from their relatives.

Some prisoners saved up their monthly allowance and wrote to their relatives offering to give them five renminbi if they would come. Naturally, when they heard the offer, the relatives were eager to visit. The guards encouraged them to take the money and admonished them to persuade the prisoners to reform their ways and confess their sins. Other prisoners knew they would never receive a visit. Unfortunately, there was a certain stigma surrounding a criminal or a counterrevolutionary that rubbed off onto the relatives, so many dared not come. Sadly, many a wife divorced her imprisoned husband to clear her name, often leaving the poor man with no one to give him medicines and food that the prison did not supply. Tragically, too, other prisoners had family members who were relocated to the countryside to "learn from the peasants," leaving the incarcerated one to suffer alone. On a happier note, most of the prisoners had loyal relatives eager to visit them. Robert knew his family was in the latter group.

Robert and his family had last seen each other on the infamous night of his arrest. Mixed feelings clouded his longing to see them again. What did they look like? A lot could happen in four years. He feared his arrest might have turned his mother's hair white with worry. What of his sister? Would her face show strain from taking care of their aging mother? As the eldest son living in Shanghai, he longed to have that responsibility again. He thought it was unfair that his sister, and not he, the rightful male provider, should have to shoulder such a burden. Surely it was too much for her. Had time treated them well? Would he recognize them?

Worse still, would they recognize him? With all the weight he had lost eating the prison diet and suffering from attacks of tuberculosis, his face was gaunt and the rest of him was but a shadow of his former self. What would they think when they saw him? Would they worry more? Deep down he knew that the desire to spend time with his relatives outweighed that fear.

Then there was the nagging question of Mary. What had happened to her? Had she met a more suitable companion? For her sake, he hoped she had. Though he loved her deeply and shuddered at the thought of losing her, he wanted what was best for her. Despite the fact that he now had a prison sentence, which meant he could project a date when they might get back together, he knew that ticking away inside every woman is a biological clock that waits for no one. Mary was no exception. It was unfair for him to expect her to wait for his release. The pressures of womanhood demanded she settle down and raise a family. Robert loved Mary so much that he wanted the best for her—even if it meant letting her go.

It occurred to him that his sentiments toward her remained much the same as when they had met upon her return from the Xinjiang Movement. At that time, he had been a pastor at risk of arrest; now he was a pastor behind bars. Hours before his arrest he had advised her not to wait for him, but she had rejected his advice. Could she wait a total of eight years for him? Had she even waited four years? If she had found a man out there beyond his prison walls who would take care of her, she deserved him. If she had not yet found such a man, he thought she should start looking. Under his present circumstances, he feared that to ask her to wait for him was selfish. In fact, it was an unreasonable request, because his prison status made him a liability. If it were known that she was still his girlfriend, his status as a counterrevolutionary could only put another black mark on her dossier. He determined that at his first visitation he would ask his sister to tell Mary to look for another man.

But there was something about Mary. He couldn't get her out of his mind. At night, when the other prisoners were asleep, he would

127

lie awake thinking about her, rehearsing the reasons why it was better for her to find someone else. While thoughts of her kept his mind active, he was tortured with anticipation. When would the visitation come?

A guard came to Robert's cell and called out the inmates' numbers. Then he handed out paper and announced, "You may write a letter to your family. We will deliver it provided it meets our approval and is not more than one hundred Chinese characters. Remember, asking for food is against the rules!" Robert stifled a gasp. With one hundred Chinese characters, he could write at the most one hundred words, but, as many words require more than one Chinese character, it was more likely to be a letter of fifty words! How could he compress four years into fifty words? It was harder than writing a composition in school.

"Letters must meet the guards' approval," the guard continued. "Choose your words carefully, or you'll be responsible for the consequences. Be positive, and repeat only facts. Don't make foolish requests!"

After the guard left, Robert thought carefully. He couldn't write anything he didn't want the guards to know. He wanted to ask whether Mary was still waiting for him, but decided against it. In a game of psychological warfare, his feelings toward her could be used as ammunition against him—or her, for that matter. It would be far better to ask his sister when she came. What could he say?

When nothing came to mind, he decided to wait.

That night, he recalled the alphabet game he had played while he had been locked in solitary confinement. It still bothered him that he had forgotten the most important J's—*Jesus* and *Jehovah*. The memory lapse revealed how greatly his faith had weakened behind bars. He wanted to get closer to Jesus and Jehovah. Besides prayer, he knew of no better way than through reading God's Word. For four years, sitting on the floor awaiting sentencing, he had been unable to even hold a Bible in his hands, let alone read one. He had tried to sustain himself by recalling scriptures he had put to memory, but it was not enough. He desperately needed a Bible to revive his spiritual strength. Silently, he asked God to help him think of a safe way to let his family know that he wanted a Bible.

There's Something About Mary

The next morning, the thoughts of the night before still rang in his mind. How could he tell his family he wanted a Bible? He prayed again for an idea.

The crackle of the loud speaker on the prison intercom interrupted Robert's prayer.

"Criminal 115, your family wants to see you. Prepare for visitation."

The crackling voice irritated Robert because it had interrupted his prayer. Try as he might, he found it impossible to get the prisoner's number out of his head. It sounded so familiar. Suddenly it dawned on him! In the Chinese hymnal, number 115 is "Give Me the Bible!"

"That's it!" he exclaimed silently. "God has answered my prayer. Now I know how to ask for a Bible!"

Instantly he called for paper so that he could write a letter to his family. After the guard had produced paper and pen and returned to his rounds, Robert sat on the floor and wrote, according to prison regulation, only one hundred Chinese characters. Deferring his desire to ask about Mary, he wrote something like this:

> Please send me a 115-page notebook. Make sure it is a 115-page notebook. If it is not a 115-page notebook I don't want it. Only send me a 115-page notebook when you visit me. Thank you for getting me the 115-page notebook. Oh, and please send me some toilet paper brand "39."

Actually, there was a toilet paper company in Shanghai that gave itself the brand name "38," but he had written "39" to represent the 39 books of the Old Testament. Would they understand? Was the wording too esoteric? Or was it openly obvious? Suddenly he worried, *Would the guards approve?* After counting the words to make sure he had not surpassed the limit, he summoned a guard, and handed him the letter.

He sat nervously as the guard read, hoping he would not see through the code. As far as Robert knew, no one published 115-page notebooks in China. Would the guard be suspicious? Eventually, after skimming over the characters on the paper, the guard grinned broadly. "I'll send this letter myself," he said.

Time passed. Robert heard more prisoners' numbers called. Other prisoners were getting to talk with their relatives; when would his turn come? If the prisoner was in a cell nearby, Robert noticed him hurriedly brushing his teeth, tidying his hair, and dressing in his best. Robert longed to be sprucing himself up, too.

Day after day, when Robert wasn't thinking about Mary, or following the routine schedule, or sharing his beliefs with his inmates, he nervously listened for his prisoner number.

After what seemed an eternity, he heard it. With less than an hour to look his best, Robert hurriedly washed up, shaved, brushed his teeth, tidied his hair, and changed into clean clothes. While he was still trying to straighten out the wrinkles in his jacket, the guard appeared. Keys rattled in the lock. Anxiously, Robert followed the guard to the visitation room.

Inside was a long, curved panel with walled compartments to separate the prisoners. Robert and the other prisoners waited for the bell. When it rang, they were to dash to their seats and visit with their relatives. They could talk until the bell rang again.

Robert observed that as the prisoners ahead of him were talking with their relatives, guards passed behind them to make sure no one broke the rules. Prisoners could not touch their family members, nor could they tell them anything negative about prison life. They were expected to say they were being treated well and relate how the prison staff was training them to fit into New China.

Robert sat and waited. Soon the visitor's door opened and to his delight, in stepped his mother and his sister. Before the bell rang, the guard let the relatives sit on the other side of the panel and reminded the guests, "No touching criminals. Guards will be listening to every word you say. You have eight minutes, so don't waste your words. If you break the rules, you will be responsible for the consequences." Turning, the guard let them sit down and then exited.

Suddenly the bell rang. Robert and the other prisoners dashed over to their seats across from their relatives.

"You have eight minutes!" the guards announced.

Eight minutes! How could families who had been separated for so many years express their emotions and relate their experiences in just eight minutes? The bell would ring before they started! Tantalizing though it was, Robert was grateful that he was allowed to see his mother and sister again.

Initially it was disconcerting to see the guards pacing behind them, but soon Robert and his family noticed that there were more prisoners than guards. It was physically impossible for them to eavesdrop on every conversation. The thought relaxed them considerably. Soon they learned to listen for the footfall of a guard and change subjects before he was within hearing range. Time ticked rapidly. While his mother and Elder Sister tried to catch him up on the outside world, Robert mostly wanted to talk about the Bible. No good opportunity to do so arose. Every time he was about to bring it up, he heard a guard approach. Had his family understood his code? If they had, why were they silent?

The other item of interest was, of course, Mary. He kept looking for an opportunity to bring her into the conversation. Why didn't his family say something about her? Had she found another man? What should he say about her? All too soon the bell rang again. Opening the guest door, a guard announced, "Time to leave!"

Neither his mother nor his sister was eager to go. The guard took them by the hand and escorted them out. As they were leaving, his sister shouted over her shoulder, "Mary says she'll wait. I sent you a package. The soap is large. Make sure you break it in two so that you won't use it up too fast." The guard pushed her out the door. Another guard stood behind Robert and called his number.

Back in his cell, his heart was filled with mixed emotions. On the one hand sadness enveloped him because he guessed that his code about the Bible had been too esoteric. Surely he had been too clever for his own good. Instead of talking about his 115-page notebook, they had only brought him a huge bar of soap. He hadn't even asked for soap! What were they thinking? On the other hand, he felt like singing as he thought of the news about Mary. She would wait!

Mary saw something in him—something valuable enough to wait for. Now, that was something! Anytime a woman loves a man enough to give herself to him, that is something. *But,* Robert thought, *when the man that a woman is willing to wait for is you, now that is* really *something.* He couldn't get the thought out of his head. A woman would wait for *him!* She would wait! Mary would *wait*! What was more, she would wait for an incarcerated counterrevolutionary. That meant she loved him even though he was sitting on the floor waiting for it to rot. *Indeed,* he thought, *there is something about Mary! If she thought he was worth waiting for, she was worth waiting for too.*

Then his mind went back to the Bible he had asked for. Why had his sister missed his request for a Bible? Was there another way he could ask for one? Or had she not given him one because she had none to give? Had the Red Guard raided their home?

Then he wondered about the soap. What had Elder Sister meant? Why did she want him to break it in two?

As his curiosity mounted, he realized that all he could do was wait for the guards to bring the gifts.

---

[1] One hundred fen equals one renminbi. At the time, three renminbi was a day's wage.

CHAPTER 20

Cracking the Soap Mystery

Hearing his number called, Robert looked up. A guard delivered a bag of gifts from his family. After taking it, Robert decided he needed some privacy. Grabbing a pan and some clothes, he prepared to do his laundry. He placed the pan against the wall so that his back would face both his cellmates and the guards. Eagerly, but with calculated nonchalance, Robert opened the bag, hoping against hope that he might find the Bible he had requested. After pulling everything out, he found only a huge bar of soap on the bottom. No Bible! No brand 39 toilet paper!

Why did they send so much soap? It wasn't even the Rainbow brand he usually requested. Why, oh why, didn't they send the Bible? Had they failed to give him a Bible because the guards had discovered it and confiscated it? Disconsolately, he examined the soap. Why had they made it so large? Why had they wanted him to halve it? Wouldn't it have been better for them to have done that themselves? Why should he break it? Why now? Why ever?

Breaking it in two did make some sense, he concluded. It would make the soap last longer. Bending over so no one would see, he pressured both sides until the bar snapped apart in the middle. Inside was a small book with thin pages. A Bible! An English-language pocket Bible! Elder Sister had hidden it in the soap to smuggle it past the guards, and they had failed to detect it. Inexpressible joy filled Robert's heart. Pocket Bibles were extremely rare in Liberated China. The government allowed only the publication of large Bibles, because it wanted to see who was carrying one. Christians could not hide their religion in their pockets as they could before the rise of Communism. Robert remembered having two pocket English Bibles in the house prior to his arrest, but he had not known if they had been confiscated. Now he could hide the whole Bible, read it, and hopefully never be discovered.

Instantly, he hid it in his underwear and then began using one half of his new soap to wash. When he had finished, he put everything away and sat in the corner of the cell nearest the bars next to the hall. Even though he knew it was the closest point of contact with the guards as they paced the hall, he thought he could best study God's Word right under their noses. None of his cellmates would want to sleep near the bars because the guards kept the light on at night. Therefore, he knew he could sleep there without ever having an argument with them. The only disadvantage was that the guards could more easily see his activities. Dangerous though it was, he was willing to take the risk in order to have light at night.

That night he set out his bedding near the bars and, once he was certain that everyone around him was asleep, rearranged his bed in such a way that he could mislead the guard into thinking he was asleep, yet enough light shone through the covers that he could read. Then he slipped out his pocket Bible, opened it, turned the pages to the light and read. He constantly listened for the footfall of the guard. Whenever he heard it approaching, he watched for the shadow of the guard's hat, and then quickly stuffed his Bible into his underwear and covered his head so the guard would not know he was awake. From under the covers, he waited until he was certain the guard had marched to the other side of the prison. Then he pulled out the Bible again and read on. This he repeated for most of the night.

The next morning the guards began shouting. Curiosity getting the better of them, Robert and the other prisoners stood near the bars, hoping to get the first glimpse of the reason for the hullabaloo. Soon a hapless criminal, his head forced to hang low to show his shame, was paraded past the cells. Around his neck he wore a string with a needle for a pendant. Guards were shouting, "His family tried to smuggle a needle into the cell in a bar of soap, but we found it. You can't fool us! We can find needles buried in soap. Don't smuggle illegal material into your cells."

Robert marveled. How had the guards found a needle hidden in that unfortunate inmate's bar of soap and yet missed an English Bible hidden in his own soap? It must have been a miracle, Robert concluded. Learning how God had helped him get his Bible gave him more courage to read at night. Surely, God wanted him to have it!

During the day, as he sat in his cell, he meditated on the verses he had read the night before and caught as many naps as possible. One of the inmates asked why he was so sleepy.

"I didn't sleep well last night," Robert equivocated. No one asked anything more. His cellmates knew from experience how difficult it could be to sleep next to a light.

Sometimes, when he went to the commode, Robert opened Chairman Mao's *Quotations* and placed his pocket Bible over the top to mislead both his cellmates and the guards. Feigning constipation, he sat and read the Bible for hours while the guards and his fellow inmates assumed he was memorizing Mao's sayings.

Based on this false impression, his cellmates often ridiculed him. "If you study Chairman Mao so much, what are you doing behind bars? If you think studying him now will do any good, you're mistaken!" they jeered. Robert ignored them and continued his prevaricative practice of secretly reading the Book that prohibits prevarication and asks the follower of Jesus to be faithful in all things, no matter what the cost—even death. So little was his faith that God had a thousand ways to protect him if it was His will. It would take time and much grief before Robert would learn that in the Christian life, one act of faith shouts louder than a thousand words.

Whenever the guards allowed some of the inmates to sit in the commons area, Robert always made sure he was the first or last to leave his cell. By being either first to arrive in the commons or last to leave his cell, he could hope to have a moment to himself with his secret Bible. He did not wish anyone—whether an inmate or a guard—to notice him pull his Bible out of his underwear. Once he was outside, he quickly looked for an empty cell. Sitting with his back to it, he slipped his pocket Bible between the pages of an open "Little Red Book" and began reading his Bible.

At night, Robert read from his Bible again. Gradually, he became almost nocturnal, but the words in the Bible renewed his strength. They were rhapsodies next to the pulp his jailers required him to read. As he read more and more from his Bible, he eventually memorized significant portions. With his spiritual cup filling to overflowing, he could not contain himself. He needed to share.

****

One day, when he was certain that the guards were pacing at the other end of the prison, Robert felt comfortable enough to ask his cellmates, "Would you like to study the Bible with me?" Tired of reading and discussing Chairman Mao all day, the other two eagerly agreed.

Not wishing to arouse the anger of the guards, Robert decided that, rather than preaching openly, it would be prudent to worship completely incognito. It had worked for him before. Surely, if he could trust his cellmates, it would work again. The only difference was that now he had a copy of the Bible from which to read directly—though he needed to translate it into Mandarin. The Bible made the study more dangerous. If a guard grew suspicious and asked to see what was going on, it was evidence that could be used against him. Thinking that he could serve the Lord longer and better if he taught in secret while appearing to comply with prison regulations, he suggested another subtle strategy.

"Let's take out our Chairman Mao's *Quotations* and pretend to read from them whenever we hear the guard approaching. But when the guard cannot see or hear what we are doing, we'll sing hymns and recite Bible texts." The others readily concurred. Taking out their "Little Red Books" they began to read. Hidden between the pages of Robert's book was his pocket Bible. Because it was too precious to be discovered, Robert felt that it still needed to be hidden from both the guards and his cellmates.

Over the next few months, they followed Robert's plan without ever arousing suspicion. Soon Robert had taught his cellmates many things in the Bible.

Cracking the Soap Mystery

Feeling haughty about his Bible-teaching success, Robert felt the outside world needed to know what he was doing in prison. How could he tell his family without spilling his secret to the guards? That was the great question that haunted him. He couldn't write a letter. If the guards read that he was preaching to his cellmates, they would be separated. That would never do. He couldn't talk about it during family visitation because a guard might overhear the conversation, and then he would be punished for proselytizing. He would have to smuggle his story to them secretly. But how?

Noticing a medicine bottle on the floor, Robert momentarily forgot his dilemma. Hastily picking it up, he hid it in his pocket, grateful that he had seen it before the guards had. Had they seen it first, they would have concluded that his sister had smuggled it in, and he would have been in trouble.

Then, as he thought about the empty bottle of medicine, an idea struck him.

CHAPTER 21

Evidence in a Bottle of Medicine

In 1969, Russia attacked China, and rumors ran rampant in the cells of Number Three Detention Center. Whispered most often was word that the prisoners would be transferred from Shanghai to somewhere along China's frontier in the western provinces. If the prisoners were transferred there, it would be almost impossible for them to see their relatives again. Few relatives could afford to take the long journey from one end of China to another. The fear that each visitation might be their last emboldened the prisoners to take risks. Robert recalled seeing a prisoner pass toilet paper to his family members unnoticed by the guard. Since nothing had happened to the man, Robert decided to try it himself. Several times he successfully passed written messages to his sister this way, unbeknownst to the guards. His success led him to believe that, despite the risks, he should try it again.

For a couple of nights, when his cellmates were asleep, Robert gradually recorded his witnessing efforts. Using only whatever beams of light came under his bed cover from the prison hallway, he began to write on toilet paper, filling each sheet without any regard to paragraphs until Chinese characters on the paper were so numerous the paper seemed to swarm with ants. Writing as often as he felt it safe to do so during those two nights, he thought back over the last four years and tried to record every attempt he had made to witness. Eventually, he determined that, though he might have forgotten one or two incidents, he had exhausted his memory.

Relieved that he had gotten his story written without arousing suspicion, he felt certain the world would want to know that in godless China, God was working through him—even in prison! Carefully, he rolled the paper scraps and hid them in the empty medicine bottle—certain that if his cellmates chanced to see it, they would never suspect its contents.

Patiently Robert waited to hear his number called for visitation. All he had to do then was look for an opportunity to pass the medicine bottle to his sister—and his story would be out.

Before he could carry out his plan, prison regulations changed. A guard appeared at Robert's cell and called for Criminal 1068—Robert's new prison number. As had happened so many times before, Robert followed the guard to the office.

The guard introduced him to an inmate. "He is one of those 'bad elements' in China, higher ranked than you, Criminal 1068," the guard sneered. "As you well know, criminals accused of being bad elements are more trustworthy than you thought-criminals. That's why you're the stinking scum of the earth." As Robert looked at an inmate ranked superior to himself, he recalled that a prisoner categorized among the "bad elements" might have been arrested for rape, murder, or theft. These crimes were considered less offensive than Robert's church activities. Criminals classified as "bad elements" were more likely to cooperate with the government, which probably explained why they were preferred.

With a broad smile, the guard interrupted Robert's thoughts by explaining, "We're organizing classes to help reform the more stubborn cases. Criminal 1068, you will be the secretary." Robert smiled. It was an honor to be chosen. It implied that he was in good standing.

The other prisoner became the group leader. The guards generally sought out thought-criminals like Robert to be secretaries because they could read and write. Robert had noticed that in his prison, criminals arrested for rape, murder, or theft could not take notes because they were almost illiterate. Mastery of at least three thousand Chinese characters is necessary to read the newspaper—a daunting feat for many too poor to attend school. Prior to China's Liberation in 1949, illiteracy was quite high. Sadly, all too often, lack of education led to lack of opportunity which, in turn, had tempted the "bad elements" to drift into crime. After seizing power from the ruling Kuomintang, the Communist regime had tried to raise the level of literacy by simplifying the Chinese characters. Unfortunately for the "bad elements" in prison, the reforms had come too late. They remained virtually illiterate. Allowing them to dictate to a thought-criminal like Robert was more practical than teaching them to read and write.

As time passed, Robert was frequently called into meetings. Guards barked instructions to the leader, and Robert dutifully wrote. Very quickly, after the guards left, the classes turned into violent struggle sessions similar to the ones he had experienced before his arrest, when the government had wanted him to attend political sessions on Sabbath. In prison, however, the "bad elements" were more cruel. The guards never actually requested the leader to physically torture fellow inmates, but it was understood. A guard might say, "This criminal is especially stubborn. Use any means necessary to obtain a change in his attitude." Perhaps the designated leaders read much more into these statements than the guards intended. When he had attended struggle sessions before his arrest, "any means necessary" could be a condescending look, a derogatory comment, or excessive peer pressure. It was different in prison. Group leaders in prison took "any means necessary" to mean hit, slap, and kick. Robert noticed that they practiced these methods only when the guards were absent.

When it was time for a meeting, the group leaders organized their groups. Each leader represented six cells, which amounted to around fifteen prisoners. After the members were seated on the floor, a guard suggested a topic for discussion, introduced an inmate to the group and pointed out his problems, then left the group leader in charge to help reform the stubborn prisoner. Inevitably, a violent struggle session ensued.

Robert wrote down everything people said and did, and then delivered the reports to the guards. Generally, the group leaders never read Robert's report. Because they had difficulty reading and writing, they relied heavily on oral instructions. Considering himself merely a stenographer, Robert made every effort to suppress his feelings and re-

Evidence in a Bottle of Medicine

main objective in his reports. In each discussion the group leader yelled out Maoist slogans. Members dutifully echoed them as they clenched their fists and threw up their arms to show their zeal. Robert was grateful to God that, as the designated court reporter, he was not expected to follow suit. He did not need to throw up his hands as much as the others. If he did, how could he report?

Being the secretary, Robert observed each prisoner's behavior carefully. Soon he discovered that criminals categorized as "bad elements" were more active in their efforts to reform prisoners than criminals described as counterrevolutionaries. When asked to hit a prisoner, "bad elements" struck the prisoners with full force, while counterrevolutionaries swung hard, but hit gently. While all the prisoners made a show of severity for the benefit of the guards and other prisoners, the counterrevolutionaries knew that someday they themselves might be in the hot seat. They hoped that their leniency might be rewarded by fellow counterrevolutionaries when their turn for reform came.

****

Hearing his number called, Robert excitedly tidied his clothes and his person. It was almost his turn for visitation. While brushing his teeth, he thought about the bottle of medicine with his story hidden inside. With the Cultural Revolution and struggle sessions fully entrenched, was this the best time to give the story to his sister? He thought about the rumors that he would be transferred to the frontier. If so, it would be far more difficult for his family to visit him. Deferring his worries, he quickly took the medicine bottle out of his pocket and held it tightly in his hand. If he were frisked, the probability that the guards would search his hand was slim.

But could he pass it to his relatives safely?

One of his cellmates returned from his visitation and said that security was tight. "I've never seen so many guards on duty during a visitation."

Robert said nothing. The news that security was tight gave him hope. As the guards had been unable to find evidence against him, he was a low-risk inmate. Likely, the guards would be more worried about other prisoners than about him. Perhaps he might be given more slack. The more Robert analyzed the situation, the more convinced he became that today was the perfect time to get his story beyond prison walls. Clenching his fist around the bottle, he felt his story was safely hidden inside.

A guard approached Robert's cell, opened the door, led him to the visitation room, and without frisking him, let him enter the room. Time moved so slowly while he waited—it seemed his relatives would never come. Eventually, the door opened and in stepped his mother and sister.

Suddenly, the bell rang, and Robert ran to his seat to meet his loved ones. During the first few minutes of the visitation the prisoners and their relatives were always sentimental. Some wailed, while others excitedly raised their voices. Many tried to break the rule banning physical contact as they reached out in desperate attempts to touch their loved ones. Understandably, emotions ran high. As families tried to make the most of their time with their relatives, many visitations were ruthlessly cut short. The guards busily enforced the rule against physical contact, which tended to cause both consternation and confusion. While the guards were keeping family members apart, they had little time to notice anything else.

Thinking he would take advantage of all the commotion, Robert stretched his hand across the table to shake hands with his sister. Forbidden though the act was, it was often winked at by the guards. While it was true that the guards made a terrific show of enforcing visitation rules, they found their task bothersome at best. Many were sympathetic, knowing that if the shoe was on the other foot, they would behave the same. Understanding this, Robert had to take the risk that the act of shaking hands with his sister, if witnessed, would be ignored this time. When he touched his sister's hand, he had the medicine bottle in his palm.

Perhaps she hesitated too long, because the act aroused suspicion. Seemingly out of nowhere, the guards swooped down, confiscated the container, canceled the visit, and pushed Robert out. He looked back and nodded farewell to his relatives, while they stood in fright.

Hurriedly, Robert was transferred to his cell. *Now*, Robert thought to himself, *would be a good time to worry about the consequences of breaking visitation rules.* If the guards discovered the message in the bottle, they would have the evidence they sought. With the Cultural Revolution in full swing, persecution was guaranteed.

The next day Robert was not called to meeting before the struggle session. When the group leader called the session to order, Robert was replaced as secretary. The guard announced, "We now have proof that Prisoner 1068, alias Criminal Huang, is against New China's military leaders. He wrote that Mr. Forest,* New China's defense minister, 'has set up the place full of idols!' " Turning to the group leader, he suggested, "For this he should be reasoned with."

The group leader shot the guard a toothy smile.

Robert knew better than to try to correct the guard. In his letter to his sister he had actually written, "There are as many idols as there are trees in a forest." It was a general statement. But the guards had given his words a political twist. Rather than risk getting himself into deeper trouble, he remained silent.

Meanwhile, the guard continued. "Criminal 1068 is a serious antireformist. He is a hardened case because he is so young and remains so stubborn. He has not only remained a Christian in prison but persists in proselytizing his fellow inmates, which is illegal. You must use whatever means necessary to persuade him to give up his God and join New China. He needs to learn that he doesn't really serve Christ but American imperialists! Convince him to admit his guilt." Before turning to go, the guard added, "No guard will beat a criminal. To do so would hurt the relationship and be counterproductive."

After the guard left, the group leader ordered, "Criminal 1068, stand up."

Robert stood.

---

* The twist is a pun in the Chinese language. The surname *Lin* means "forest" in Chinese. In this case, "Mr. Forest" was Lin Piao, the ill-fated designated successor to Chairman Mao, who disappeared shortly after a failed attempt to assassinate the Chairman and take over the government by force. It is said he died in a plane crash in Mongolia. Supposedly he was trying to escape China after the unsuccessful coup. Not a few prisoners in Shanghai were convicted of crimes after their arrest based upon their loyalty or disloyalty to this Party member who fell from grace. If the prisoner was loyal to "Mr. Forest" before he had been disgraced, he was considered one of "Forest's" accomplices, which was evidence that the prisoner was antiParty.

"So you're a preacher! Don't you know that because you continue to preach in jail, you're not only violating the rules, but you're also continuing to carry out your counterrevolutionary activities behind bars?"

At a signal by the group leader, some of the inmates beat Robert. One blow struck Robert's glasses, breaking them and sending them flying across the room. Without them Robert's world was a blur.

"Bend over!" the group leader shouted.

Robert complied.

Turning to the others, the group leader instructed, "If you think his head is not bent down far enough, then help him." Instantly, one of the prisoners arose and pounded Robert's head downward until he was bowing from the waist at a right angle. "Good!" he exclaimed. Looking over to where the secretary sat, the group leader looked pleased to see him writing. Turning back to Robert, he added, "Remain in that position, Criminal 1068, until you give up your God. Now," the group leader addressed the others, "ask Criminal 1068 whom he serves."

Almost as one voice, the others demanded to know, "Whom do you serve?"

"I serve God," Robert replied.

They asked, "And whom does God serve?"

"God serves the people. He serves the whole world."

"You serve American imperialism." Then, quoting Lenin, they said, "The role of the pastor is the same as that of an executioner!"

This went on continuously from morning until evening for nearly two weeks. Sometimes Robert was deprived of sleep. He was forced to kneel for long periods. He used the time to pray, but whenever his eyes closed, he was beaten mercilessly. They quoted Chairman Mao, claiming that he, Criminal 1068, would "carry a granitelike skull to see God." It meant Robert was stubborn and incorrigible. They kicked him and hit him with their fists and their shoes. One particularly severe kick to his chest cracked a rib, causing searing pain and putting him in agony when he was forced to stand and bend over. Repeated blows to his face made it swell. One evening, when he was allowed to return to his cell, he could not recognize himself in the window.

When his food was served the next day, Robert discovered it contained minced pork. It was the second time they had canceled his status that allowed him to eat steamed vegetables and the *halal* diet. *Why are they testing me on this issue again?* he wondered. That day he did not eat. Without food it was more difficult for him to stand with his body bent at the waist, but, with God's help, he managed.

Fortunately, pork was not served daily, so Robert ate heartily the next day.

A few days later the police encouraged some prisoners to harass Robert. "Handcuff his hands behind his back," the police suggested, handing them a pair of handcuffs. Eagerly, the prisoners obeyed. Robert instantly felt violated, though he kept his feeling to himself. If they could handcuff him, they could search his body and all his belongings. Then they might discover his pocket Bible!

Sadly, like the children of Israel in the wilderness in Moses' day, Robert forgot how Elder Sister had smuggled him his Bible inside a bar of soap. He also forgot that the same guards who had found a needle in another bar of soap had miraculously been unable to find the Bible hidden in his. Instead of trusting that God had a thousand ways to protect him, Robert worried that it was too dangerous for him to keep his Bible hidden in his underwear.

Rather than exercising his faith in his Savior, he worried that, if the Bible were found, the beatings would increase. Worse still, Robert reasoned, the discovery of the Bible would be proof that his family had smuggled illegal contraband into the prison. Both he and his family would get into trouble. The police might raid Elder Sister's house and discover other Bibles. Robert did not want her to suffer increased hardship.

He worried less about the consequences for himself than the trouble he might cause others. After all, he had already been arrested, so he couldn't be arrested again. All the guards could do was taunt him, hit him, and beat him. However, it was a very different story with his sister. She lived in constant fear of being arrested. If his Bible were discovered, Robert thought, her arrest would be certain. It was an event he felt obliged to prevent.

Seeking to solve the problem himself instead of waiting to discover God's plan, Robert decided he must dispose of his precious Bible.

CHAPTER 22

Flushing God Down the Drain

The interrogations in the struggle sessions dragged on for five months. During this time Robert had only one respite. A friend of his was brought to trial, and Robert was summoned to court to testify. After being forced to stand in an awkward position for weeks, Robert enjoyed sitting in a comfortable chair for the duration of the trial. He said nothing against his friend except to verify that he was indeed a Christian. When it was over, Robert was again the center of attention in his struggle session. Some days he was deprived of sleep as he was forced to stand bent at the waist. Day after day, at the group leader's suggestion, the inmates taunted him as they beat him.

"You believe in God?" they barked one day. "You think He can help you. Then why hasn't He helped you?" Suddenly, a fist connected solidly against his chest, and Robert felt searing pain. "I just hit you!" an inmate shouted. "Your God didn't do anything about it! Is your God for real?"

The words troubled Robert greatly. Where was God in his time of trial? Had God abandoned him? Had he committed some sin for which he had neglected to request forgiveness?

Even though he harbored many doubts in his heart, Robert kept them deep inside. To such taunts he said nothing. His face remained expressionless.

Flushing God Down the Drain

When he did not reply, the group leader grew tired and demanded that Robert kneel. Gladly, he obeyed. While inmates kicked and beat him, Robert closed his eyes and prayed. His lips must have moved. One of the inmates discovered he was praying and pointed it out to the team leader.

"Stand!" he shouted as he kicked Robert in the back. Pain shot through his spinal column as Robert stood. "Bow!" the team leader yelled, smacking Robert behind the head. "Show some humility!"

Robert bowed.

"Lower!"

Robert complied.

"Lower!"

Robert obeyed and found himself staring at the floor. Bent from the waist, he was forced to stand for hours. Uncomfortable though he was, he made the best of the situation by considering himself bowing before his Maker. Closing his eyes, he prayed. In time, however, Robert found standing in this position excruciatingly more painful than kneeling. Generally, he suffered in silence.

One day, however, he grew tired of the taunts and decided to teach his tormentors something about Christianity. While still bent with his face toward the floor, he asked, "Did you know that Jesus Christ was a carpenter? That means he was a proletarian!"

They were stymied. No one had ever told them that before. Momentarily they stood in silence as if begging him to tell them more.

Robert obliged. "Throughout his life, Jesus was always sympathetic toward the proletariat. His life was not that of a bourgeoisie. He was born in a stable and didn't have a place to lay his head. His upbringing fits into the Communist ideology."

Robert wondered whether his words had reached any of them. He couldn't be sure, but he liked to think that deep down some of them may have listened. None of the prisoners could reveal their hearts. Most masked their feelings during the struggle sessions, just as Robert did.

His respite from torture ended almost as quickly as it had begun, and Robert fell into silence again. Closing his eyes, he prayed that God would prevent the guards from discovering his Bible. He asked God to help him think of a safe place to hide it where it could never be traced to him. Then he came up with a plan, but to carry it out would be very dangerous. Soon the struggle session ended for the day and Robert and the inmates were escorted back to their respective cells.

After suffering silently for several more days, Robert, tired of their torment, spoke up again in one of the struggle sessions. "Did you know that some Marxist beliefs are compatible with Christianity?"

A prisoner in the struggle session jeered, "Tell us!"

Looking the jeering prisoner in the eye, Robert answered, "The Bible says, 'He who does not work shall not eat.' That's what Communists teach, isn't it?" Turning his head to look toward the other members of the group, he thought he might have seen a hint of agreement in some of their eyes. Robert continued, "The Bible also says that 'everyone should work as he is able.' Actually," he added, "this Marxist idea originated with the early Christian Jews and is documented by Luke in the book of Acts. In fact, Marx himself was a German Jew. Although he rejected God, he still incorporated many Judeo-Christian ideas into his utopian society."

Momentarily, the other members stood silent as if digesting Robert's words and then one shouted, "Lies! Marx taught that religion was the opiate of the people! He's telling lies!"

Others joined in. The beating and taunting resumed. On the surface, the inmates categorically rejected Robert's comments.

Outwardly, Robert never gave up his belief in God. He never said anything against his Savior. Strong though he seemed to be, deep down in his heart he was struggling. He questioned his efforts to witness in his cell. Had he been right to risk all by proudly trying to tell his story to the outside world? Hadn't he been foolish to risk his life by trying to pass a note to his sister?

Why had he even tried to witness in the first place? What was the value of witnessing? Every time a new prisoner was placed in his cell and Robert talked about the Bible with him, he gave a poor Judas another opportunity to report on him.

Was it worth it?

Wouldn't it have been easier to have left his fellow inmates to their fate? Surely they had rejected Christ or they wouldn't be locked up. In time, while he was being beaten on all sides, he began to wonder whether it was better to keep his religion to himself.

Flushing God Down the Drain

Convinced though he was about the merits of obeying China's ban on proselytizing, he kept his opinions to himself. Instead he stood firm and refused to give up his Savior when asked.

However, he debated whether it was wise to resist the authorities on all points. The beatings grew worse, and pork seemed to be served more frequently. On the days that he did not eat in order to avoid eating pork, he felt weak from hunger. Having given in to eating pork once before, the temptation was strong to do so again. In his weakened condition, he forgot how difficult it had been to persuade the guards to serve him just steamed vegetables again. As the torture continued, he worried about his health.

Should he compromise again? he asked himself frequently. Fearing that his tuberculosis might return, he rationalized that God might expect him to eat pork to build up his strength. Certainly he would be better able to stand for hours if his stomach were full. Though his resolve was weakening, still he resisted. Closing his eyes, he prayed, "Lord, if it is Your will, I will lay down my life in torture here. I pray not for me. Instead I pray for my family and for the church members who were under my care in Shanghai. Please, Lord, don't let them be hurt on account of anything I have done."

The daily taunts from the other cellmates rang in his ears. "If your God is real, why can't He protect you from us? Why hasn't He struck us down for persecuting you?"

His body in torment and his mind in anguish, Robert began to doubt that God could protect his family and his church members. If He had not demonstrated His power through a miracle to protect him from his antagonists, how could he know that God would protect his family or the church members to whom he had ministered?

If you die, it will be useless, Robert thought to himself in his weaker moments. *Worse still, your Bible will surely be found. Then woe on your family!* It seemed that only he could protect his family and the church members. Wasn't there something to the old adage that "God helps them who help themselves"?

Momentarily forgetting that God had promised to provide a way of escape from every temptation, Robert hoped to earn a respite from his pain and suffering by solving the problem himself. After all, wasn't he worth more alive than dead? In death he would cause suffering to all whom he loved. He did not want that. Without trusting God to solve the problem in His own time, Robert decided that some sort of compromise was necessary.

Because he had surrendered to this line of reasoning once before, it was easier for him the second time. When the next serving of pork arrived on his plate, Robert ate it.

Once his compromise was observed, his tormentors praised him. They seemed to refrain from beating and taunting him as severely. Sadly, however, the respite was short-lived. Soon they demanded that he adapt more.

When he was forced to bow in the next struggle session while those around him jeered and beat him, Robert expected the pork would help him feel stronger. Instead he felt more like Adam and Eve after eating the forbidden fruit. He discovered that he preferred hunger pains to battling with a compromised conscience. Unfortunately, having started to eat pork again, he found stopping difficult. Soon his conscience quieted down, and he ate it whenever it was served. He learned that his compromise was futile. Under the encouragement of the guards, the members in his struggle sessions became even more merciless in their demands that he join New China by denying that God exists.

Whether he compromised on his diet or not, Robert was certain of one thing. He would not deny that his Savior lives!

No matter how fierce the authorities' tactics became, Robert did not convert to the socialist way. Seeing that their efforts were fruitless, the authorities altered their strategy. At the beginning of a session, a guard pulled out a list of names, ordered Robert to read the names aloud and handed him the paper. When Robert received the list, he saw that those on it had been sentenced to be executed. As he read the list to the members, he considered it a hint. Were they saying, "If he doesn't mend his ways, he may be on the next list"? Thinking his death might be near, Robert thought about his Bible. If the guards were punishing him this severely for passing a note to his sister, how would they react if they found the Bible? If they frisked him, they would find it in his underwear, and then he was certain the floodgates of tribulation would engulf both him and his family.

Flushing God Down the Drain

Surely, if they had proof that he and his family had smuggled contraband on other occasions, he might be beaten to death. He did not want his sister to be forced to pay for the bullet that had killed him.

After being forced for several days in a row to read lists of prisoners sentenced to be executed, Robert felt certain that the exercise was intended as a veiled threat on his life. The worst list was that of fifty prisoners who were executed on a single day. Two on the list had been Christians martyred for their faith. It was clear that both prisoners and guards were watching his every step. He reasoned that the guards were waiting for an excuse. His fears were substantiated when he was forced to fast two or three times a week. With three more years on his prison sentence, Robert wondered how much longer his body could withstand the malnutrition. Many times he wondered why he hadn't already been executed. Certainly, if he were to make one misstep, or if the guards were to discover an additional secret activity, it would be curtains for him. Fortunately, unless one of his inmates reported, there was no new evidence. The only problem, he feared, was his Bible.

One day Robert and the other prisoners were allowed to go to their prison lockers. Robert seized the opportunity to hide his Bible in his assigned locker. The lockers were commonly used for storing soap and detergent for laundry.

Having successfully hidden it, Robert began to worry. Usually, the guards left the lockers alone, but they might raid it for evidence. Chiding himself for his foolishness, he soon regretted having placed the Bible in his locker. If they found the Bible, Robert did not want to imagine the results. He began to think his pocket Bible was his baby Moses. It couldn't be safely hidden forever. But how could he dispose of it?

Carefully he considered every option. The lockers were not safe because they were inspected periodically. Because it was impossible for prisoners to step outside the building, Robert considered the well in the commons area. Knowing that he was being watched carefully, he kept his eye on the well and discovered that it, too, was inspected. The situation was the same for the manure pit. The only place that the guards did not inspect was the commode, but Robert hated to throw God's Word into such a place. Keeping it in his locker had been a foolish decision. He determined to get it out of his locker before the guards did. All he needed was a good opportunity. He waited and prayed.

The opportunity came suddenly and unexpectedly. The guards announced, "Criminals, listen up! Get your dirty clothes together. We will permit you scoundrels to wash them in the commons area." Unable to believe his good fortune and certain that it was God's answer to his prayer, Robert made sure that he was one of the first to get to the lockers. When he felt certain that no one was watching, he wrapped his Bible in plastic, snatched it out of his locker, rolled it up in his dirty laundry and stuck it all into his wash basin.

Dashing to the courtyard, he was one of the first prisoners to arrive. Carefully scouting for the best location, he selected a spot behind a rock that was near a huge drainage outlet. Sitting with his face to the wall and the rock to his back, he began soaping his laundry into a lather. When he felt no one was looking, he pushed his Bible into the outlet. A return current pushed the Bible back. Hastily, before he might arouse suspicion, he thrust it back into the drain. Closing his eyes, he prayed, "Lord, it is too risky for me to keep my Bible. Its discovery would cause great harm to those I love. Please take it away from me. Watch over it and help someone find it who will be blessed by it." This time it flowed away, and Robert felt God had answered his prayer.

For a short time Robert had one less worry during the struggle sessions, but soon he was filled with remorse. He had flushed his Bible down a drain! The horror of his deed depressed him. His precious Bible was gone forever. With each passing day, he missed it more and more. Truly, he had fallen short of the glory of God. He chided himself for not trusting enough. Why had he tried to solve his problems his own way? Hadn't God performed a miracle to keep the guards from finding his smuggled Bible? Hadn't the guards found a needle in a bar of soap on the very day that his family had smuggled in his Bible? If the guards had been unable to discover his Bible when they were inspecting his soap, certainly God could have prevented them from finding it in his locker. If only he had let God be God, he would still have his precious Book. He determined to obtain another one, but, with his every move under constant scrutiny and his family visits banned, it would not be easy.

Flushing God Down the Drain

Meanwhile, the struggle sessions continued, and with them came the taunts and the beatings. Robert's case had become well known in the prison. Inmates in other cells knew he was a Christian and demanded he give up his superstitious belief in God. Robert stopped listening.

One day, as he was limping his way down the hall toward his cell, Robert chanced to meet Mr. Ho Shan, a young man with whom he had once shared a cell. At the time, the young man had been eager to learn about Christianity. He had listened to Robert's Bible stories and had seemed to respect him. When their eyes met on this occasion, Robert knew instantly that things had changed. Hysterically, in a sarcastic tone, Ho Shan shouted, "You're not a true Christian. If you were really brave and kept your faith, you wouldn't have eaten pork!"

Hearing the words pierced Robert's heart like an arrow. The words hurt worse than all the blows he had felt over the last few months. It occurred to him that, like David in the Bible, this young man was Shimei cursing his king when he was fleeing from Absalom. God was sending him a message through this young man's sarcasm.

Robert knew that he could not obtain salvation through his diet. Paul clearly stated in Hebrews that people are saved through an active faith in Jesus Christ. But obviously, God was judging Robert's faith by his diet. Just as He had placed a tree of forbidden fruit in the garden as a test of loyalty for Adam and Eve, He was now testing Robert's faith when the guards offered him pork. By eating the pork, Robert had not just compromised with the authorities; he had also compromised his witness as a Christian. Though he felt physically weak in the next struggle session, spiritually he compared himself to Samson at the gristmill. When he had eaten his first bite of pork in prison, Robert sensed that his proverbial hair had been cut. He was like Samson who had compromised with Delilah and lost his hair. Without it, Samson could not fulfill God's plan for his life. By eating pork, Robert realized, he too had strayed from God's ideal plan for his life.

God had another message for him. He accidentally met Ho Shan in the hall again. Looking at Robert's drooping shoulders, Mr. Ho shouted, "Jesus was raised on the cross so His back was straight."

Robert realized his slouched posture revealed his spiritual state. He had grown so discouraged in prison that he had forgotten to stand firm for God. If he continued in his self-pity, it would lead him to eternal death. He had to stand tall—even under torment. As he walked the rest of the way to his cell, Robert prayed, "God, I am like Samson pushing the gristmill. Without his hair and his eyes, he could clearly see his weak spiritual condition and learned to depend upon You. My hair has also been cut, and I have been blind to my spiritual weaknesses. Please, help my hair to grow back quickly. Renew my strength so that I can stand straight again and become a mighty warrior for You."

Doubts rushed through his mind. He knew he was weak and questioned whether he could withstand the remorse he felt because he had compromised his beliefs. He prayed again, "Lord, save me! Let my weakness be Your strength. Exchange my filth with Your holiness. You are my righteousness, my sanctification, my redemption, my wisdom, and my life." Still he could not muster the courage to tell the guards he wanted to be served *halal*. Chinese are reluctant to challenge authority, and Robert was no exception. Forgetting the fact that God's authority was higher than that of the guards, he felt too timid to protest. His proverbial hair was still too short.

Then he recalled a member of the Yiguandao who was imprisoned because the Chinese government considered the Yiguandao to be a reactionary secret society that had, under the guise of religion, served the Japanese invaders and Kuomintang. The prisoner had refused to eat meat of any kind, was suspicious of every meal, and fasted. The guards exhausted every method, even handcuffing him, nasal feeding him, and threatening to force-feed him, but he refused to eat. His body had wasted away to the point that he was a living skeleton. Even though Robert did not agree with the prisoner's ideas, he admired him. If this man could stand firm on his own strength, Robert thought, why couldn't he, with God's help, follow the example of the Yiguandao? Still, as long as the struggle sessions continued, he hesitated to request a Muslim diet. It had taken only one day for Jesus' parents to lose him in the temple, and it was three days before they found him again. Like Joseph and Mary, Robert found himself wandering three allegorical days as he retraced his steps toward Jesus. Truly, his spirit was willing, but his flesh was weak. He knew what he needed to do, but he was reluctant to follow through.

Flushing God Down the Drain

****

Without notice, almost as quickly as they had been formed, the struggle sessions suddenly stopped. No explanation was given. The threats against Robert's life ceased, and he again sat in his cell serving his sentence. But the criticism of antireformists continued. The guards ordered antireformists and activists to attend "educational" programs in the prison auditorium. Robert, being an antireformist, was forced to attend. In one program, the highest ranking military officer controlling the prison criticized various kinds of reactionary ideas, including religion. With his nose high in the air, he strutted around the prisoners as proud as a peacock, denouncing God. Among the thousands of prisoners in attendance, all were as mute as fish.

Suddenly, the officer pointed his finger, called a prisoner's number, and demanded, "You stand up!"

Thousands of eyes focused on one lone prisoner known to be a Catholic priest.

With his head held high, the chief military officer asked, "Do you still believe in God?"

A deathly silence followed.

Then the priest replied in a clear voice, "Yes, I do."

Robert no longer heard the ranting of the military officer. He was excited by the priest's answer. Robert, like Elijah when he fled from the wrath of Jezebel, had almost convinced himself that he was the last Christian in Shanghai. This assumption had weakened him. Now he knew he was not alone. With him in the same prison was a fellow inmate who not only believed in God but proudly proclaimed it. His words had rung in everyone's ears. God used him as a tower of strength to encourage Robert. Among the thousands of reactionaries there stood a dazzling diamond. Like Nebuchadnezzar, the military officer blew his own trumpet, but one person stood loyal to God. The priest was a modern-day Shadrach, who was willing to go to the burning fiery furnace if necessary to give glory to God.

Mingled with Robert's excitement was a feeling of shame that he had not rebuked the military officer before the Catholic priest. And shame that he had not yet requested a Muslim diet. He longed to follow the priest's example, but as long as he was eating pork, he considered himself a hypocrite. With the eyes of others focused on him, his hypocrisy kept him from witnessing for his faith. What of those who might call him Mr. Legality for refusing to eat pork? True, he could not be saved by diet alone, but through God's grace, which would enable him to eat healthfully. He knew his first stand should be to show everyone that he was living his faith and not just preaching it. Yet he hesitated, unwilling to surrender his all on this point. Hadn't God abandoned him during his time of suffering? Hadn't he needed to eat the pork to survive the ordeal? As he struggled to act on his convictions, the example of the priest's active faith gave him a moment to pause.

The plight of Robert's younger brother came to mind. In one of his last visitations, his family told him of his brother's arrest and subsequent incarceration in a hard-labor camp. Two black marks were on his dossier. He was a doctor and a Christian. Because peasants and factory workers were in favor, doctors and professionals were the scum of the earth. He was arrested because he was a doctor and persecuted behind bars because he was a Christian. In one visitation his family attempted to tell Robert that his brother was standing firm in his faith. Difficult though it was to talk when they were under the watchful eye of the guard, they had been able to say, "No matter how great his suffering, your brother has not compromised himself." Proud of his brother, Robert wondered what his brother would say to him if he continued to eat pork. But still he resisted challenging the guard's authority.

The "educational program" ended and the prisoners returned to their cells. With the conclusion of the program, Robert soon forgot the ranting of the officer. All Robert could remember was the priest's witness. Over the next few days Robert's conscience nagged him constantly. The influence of the priest and his brother was very strong. Robert found it increasingly difficult to kick against the pricks of a guilty conscience. As he meditated upon his plight, a scratchy voice over the intercom interrupted him. Straining hard to catch the words, Robert realized it was an announcement from the women's quarters. "Even now," the announcer stated, "someone is praying in her cell."

Robert could barely contain his excitement. Hearing that God had a witness in another section of the prison made Robert determined to stand firm regardless of the results. Here was a woman whom he had never met, witnessing in her cell. Indeed, he was not the only Christian in his prison. At least two others were refusing to hide their faith. Though they were fireflies in a jar, they were still shining! If they could be strong, why couldn't he?

Unfortunately, Robert's Bible was gone. He could no longer search it for answers to his problems. However, he prided himself that he had read it through six times before flushing it down the drain. He had committed large portions of God's Word to memory. A promise came to his mind from Psalm 37: "Though he stumble, he will be made firm; for the Lord upholds him with His hand." Robert claimed it, and his faith soared with the eagles. Like Samson's hair growing back, Robert could feel renewed strength.

Mr. Ho Shan's words rang in his ears as if he had said them yesterday: "If you were a true Christian, you wouldn't have eaten pork!" Robert decided that he could not be a stumbling block for anyone else.

The next time he was served pork, Robert again requested to eat *halal*. When the guards refused to comply, Robert fasted. Now that he was again refusing to eat it, his "hair," like Samson's, was growing back, and with it his spiritual strength was renewed. The guards tested Robert's resolve for a time, and then eventually served him steamed vegetables and a Muslim diet.

As Robert's spiritual strength grew back, so did his confidence. Soon, as other prisoners noted the change in him, Robert became fearless in his witness for his Savior.

CHAPTER 23

And God Defied Gravity

After deciding to quit eating pork, Robert grew closer to his Lord. Persuading the guards that he meant to put his beliefs into action strengthened his character. As he grew stronger in his own spirituality, he felt emboldened to share his faith with his cellmates. Still afraid to witness openly, he shared his faith secretly. He told the inmates Bible stories, taught them hymns, and shared some of his own spiritual poetry with them. In the four years after his sentencing, he suffered many hardships, but his Savior revealed himself in miraculous ways.

One day, not long before September 29, 1972, the day Robert was scheduled to be released, he was called into the office. After he sat across from the officer, who asked, "Criminal 1068, do you still believe in God?"

Robert said he did.

"Do you still pray?"

"Yes."

"How many times a day?"

Initially, Robert was at a loss for words. How should he answer? Actually, he followed Paul's advice and prayed without ceasing, but would the officer understand if he told him he prayed all day long? Surely ceaseless praying would make no sense to a Marxist, Robert thought. He could have answered that he prayed once a day, which would have been true, though misleading. Somehow he thought the answer would need a lengthy explanation that the officer wouldn't understand. How could he answer? To simplify the issue, he prevaricated, saying, "Five times."

Hearing the answer, the officer grew red in the face, slammed his fist on the table, and shouted, "You haven't been reformed yet. Because you refuse to reign in your stubborn horse, you alone are responsible for the results of your actions. I don't think you deserve to be released. Instead, we'll send you to a labor camp. Go back to your room, sit on the floor, and await further orders."

His day for release passed without instructions from the jailers, but Robert did not lose heart. September 25 comes so close to Liberation day, October 1, that prisoners scheduled to be released then would expect to wait until October 10 or 11 to be transferred.

On October 10, 1972, about three years after the struggle sessions, Robert was released from prison—only to be transferred to a hard-labor camp. He joined ten other prisoners as they climbed into the back of a large blue truck. Because they were no longer prisoners, no one handcuffed them; however, they were under armed guard. The driver took them to an industrial site about an hour's drive outside Shanghai on the far side of the Whampoa River. Most counterrevolutionary prisoners like Robert who were transferred from prison to labor camps were not sent to camps located anywhere near their homes. Robert was the only Seventh-day Adventist minister arrested who was placed close to home. Why was he being treated with such lenience? He was the son of an American. He was also a young minister without a family of his own. He had a mother and an elder sister but no wife and children. Was it because he was *wai kiu* that he stayed near Shanghai? Was God leading him into a relationship with Mary, from whom he had been separated?

The prisoners transferred with Robert begged the guards to give them permission to return home. They had been released from prison, they argued, and wanted to visit their relatives before commencing their duties in the labor camp. Ultimately the guards granted the request. Soon Robert and the other ten inmates were standing on a street corner—free! Free for only a three-day weekend, that is, but free none the less. It had been many years since they had lost their freedom. For Robert it had been just over eight years. Unmindful of his short hair and wasted countenance, he felt euphoria. It was as though he were a deer rushing out from the zoo into the forest.

At first he was afraid to cross the street. After spending eight years sitting on the floor all day, the cars, trucks, and bicycles seemed as swift as the wind. Staying on the sidewalk, he came to a bus stop. Fearfully he climbed onto a bus and then a ferry toward home.

How he anticipated going home! To sit in a chair in his living room and talk without worrying whether anyone was listening would be a luxury. He wondered what had happened to his church members. Had they remained faithful? He longed to minister to them again.

And then there was Mary. Did he want to see her again? He wasn't sure. How long would he need to serve in the labor camp? It didn't seem fair to ask her to wait any longer. She should forget about him and find someone else.

And then, at last, after what seemed like an incredibly slow trip, there in front of him was home. Untold joy and anticipation shot through his veins. After dashing up the three flights of stairs, with his heart pounding furiously, he knocked on the door. Would they be home? Would Mary be there? What would she look like? How would they react when they met?

Seeing him standing outside, Elder Sister flung the door wide and called her mother, who came quickly to the door.

"Robert, is it really you?" she exclaimed.

"*Shur da! Shur da!*" Robert shouted in Mandarin. "Sure! Sure! It's me! I'm home!"

"We want you to stay forever!"

"I'll need to return to the camp on Monday."

"You're here for the weekend!" Excitedly the family welcomed him inside.

Sitting in the living room on the big wooden chair, Robert related his prison experience. They were grateful that they could talk openly. Robert shared how he had used 153, one of his prison numbers, as a means to witness, and then he suggested that they sing hymn number 153, "All the Way My Savior Leads Me." As he sang, tears of joy ran down his cheeks. When they finished singing, Robert asserted, "My Savior has indeed led me all the way through my prison experience.

And God Defied Gravity

And I know He will continue to lead me through whatever lies ahead for me in the hard-labor camp!"

A knock on the door interrupted them. Uncertain who it might be, they checked. It was Mary.

"As soon as I learned Robert was in town, I rushed over immediately. I want to hear what happened in prison."

Robert's eyes met Mary's, and she beamed. It was the first time they'd been together for eight years. Robert thought that she looked more mature than before. But the radiance in her eyes shone so clearly that Robert knew there was still something special about her.

However, because he was classified as a stinking counterrevolutionary, Robert did not want to become involved with her. Nagging at him was his old worry that she would be given another black mark on her dossier on account of him. She was already suffering because her reactionary father had been sent to "learn from the peasants" in Anwi; she didn't deserve more trouble. When he thought about his shaven head, he felt very self-conscious around her. Invisible though it was, he still wore a "counterrevolutionary hat" that all could see if they asked for his identity papers. Because they were typed with black ink, everyone knew he was a prisoner. Though he had been freed from the detention center, he was bound to a hard-labor camp, which made him a member of the lowest class in New China's classless society. He concluded that Mary deserved another man, one better than he. How could he, someone serving time in a labor camp, support himself—let alone a wife?

His resolve weakened when she sat beside him on the couch. Gazing into Mary's lovely eyes as she spoke so sweetly to him, his heart conflicted with his intellect. His head knew everything was wrong, but his heart thought everything felt very right.

She had waited so long! Clearly she had demonstrated her love, and he wanted to return it. He felt confused. Was God guiding them down a road they would share?

Can she read my thoughts? he wondered.

Why was he so hesitant to express his true feelings? As he gazed upon her after the years of separation, she looked better than he had imagined. Her eyes glowed as only a woman's eyes can in the presence of the man she loves.

Their first words were to thank God for His love and that He had allowed Robert to return safely home. Sensing Robert's dilemma, Mary said, "Elder Sister found a poem you wrote fourteen years ago when Father was arrested and I was in Xinjiang. In it you expressed your feelings of sympathy, love, and best wishes for me." Robert remembered when his sister had told him about the letter in a prison visitation. Too shy to send the poem himself, he'd kept his new-found love a secret then. Understanding the situation, his sister, without asking his permission, had wisely passed it along.

"When Elder Sister showed me the letter," Mary continued, "I was deeply touched." Smiling, Robert recalled the happiness he'd felt when he learned Mary had appreciated the letter. The news had sustained him many days in detention. "Your poem helped me maintain my resolve to wait for you no matter what might happen," Mary said. "Now today we meet again."

Hearing the words, Robert knew Mary did not mind his lowly condition. She was waiting for a person whom she cared deeply about even after a long separation. There was much he wanted to say, but he kept his thoughts to himself. Seven years after his arrest on September 28, 1964, Robert had begun to think of Mary as his Rachel. Like Jacob, who had waited seven years for Rachel's hand, Robert thought Mary was worth every day of the wait. During those years, prison walls had separated them. The guards never permitted her to visit him, yet they never prevented her from sending gifts. She sent products with brand names that expressed her feelings—brands like Long Rainbow, Green Leaf and Dove, but Robert's favorite brand was Deer. Receiving a Deer product always warmed his heart. Though they were separated by prison walls, news about her kept Robert and Mary close.

Mary broke the silence again. "The first time I saw you was when you spoke in church," she said. "I prayed in my heart, 'God, if it is Thy will, make him my good companion.' " She paused to let the meaning of the words sink in, and then added, "I only want love."

How could he hurt her noble feelings with his hesitation? Though he had often given her the freedom to find another partner, how could he resist her love? Love that had persisted and had grown in expectations. Robert felt that patient love tried in suffering deserved reward. *Wouldn't now be a good time to ask for her hand in marriage?* he wondered. Prudence dictated otherwise. He couldn't afford to be married. The truth of the matter was, with his meager wage at the labor camp, he could hardly afford to be single. Why should he make matters worse by taking a wife?

Something kept him from sharing his true feelings. For the time being, Robert thought, the words of the poem would have to suffice.

After three days at home, Robert reported to the local police station and returned to the labor camp.

****

For his first assignment, Robert was ordered to pick away at rock in a granite quarry. Three days later, he and two coolies were ordered to unload boats transporting twenty-seven tons of dolomite and granite to be smelted into glass and made into windows. Ships sailed down a river that ran through the grounds to the center of the industrial site and delivered their loads.

On the boat, Robert and his partner used metal tongs to pick up a hundred-pound stone block and place it in a basket. Other workers around him picked up the granite blocks as if they were pumice, but Robert could not. With difficulty, Robert and his co-worker repeated the process until they had two or three blocks in the basket. Noticing Robert's struggles, his partner, a wiry, muscular coolie, kindly suggested that Robert take the lead. "It's easier for beginners," he explained with a smile. "The one who guides doesn't carry as much of the weight." Gratefully, Robert agreed. After sliding a pole under a rope attached to the basket loaded with hand-hewn stones, they each picked up the pole and placed an end on their shoulders.

Burdened with a 250-pound load, Robert discovered that walking with the grace of a coolie was not as easy as it looked. Naturally uncoordinated, he staggered toward the narrow gangplank between the boat and the dock. His clumsiness forced his partner to shoulder more than his share of the weight.

Once the blocks were off the ship, he worked with the other men to stack them neatly. Difficult though the task was, Robert did amazingly well at first. But gradually his years of sitting on the floor began to show their effect.

By the third day, his legs trembled under the load. The other inmates sported bulging muscle and calluses on their shoulders, but Robert's muscles—what few he once had—had atrophied in the detention center. After several trips that day, he was out of breath. The pole was eating into his flesh. His shoulders ached. To ease the pain, he lifted the pole slightly with his hands. Sweat stung his shoulder and poured down his back.

Robert felt that every eye was fixed upon him. By holding the pole in his hand, he must have been quite conspicuous. Surely, he thought, his broken horn-rimmed glasses made him even more of a spectacle.

Indeed, some guards noticed him and jeered, "You've never carried a load in your life. You're just a despicable 'intellectual.' " Soon they were chuckling and calling attention to him as he wobbled along, still holding the pole above his shoulder. "Look at that counterrevolutionary. Just like all the rest of them, he's obviously never worked a day in his life."

Hearing the guard's jests, others looked and laughed also. Before long, the laughter seemed to have spread throughout the quarry. It seemed to Robert—and to those around him—that he was all thumbs. Many sneered, "See how useless an education is!"

His feeble legs shook. Staggering toward the gangplank, he somehow managed to put one foot in front of the other. He even managed to wobble onto the plank. But then, distracted by the taunting, Robert stumbled. His legs collapsed, and his glasses disappeared.

He felt himself falling. Before he could catch a breath, he hit the water with a mighty splash, reinforced by the granite boulders that slid from the basket and tumbled in after him.

Down he sank, deeper and deeper into the canal. All he could think about was being trapped under those huge blocks. Drowning was not how he had expected his life to end.

Even without his glasses, he could see murky images around him. Looking up, he saw, to his surprise, that the blocks of granite were no longer directly above him. *How could that be?* he thought. *Is there a slight current in the canal, or did my angel push the stones aside?* A few seconds later, as the laws of gravity dictate, both he and the stones hit the bottom at almost exactly the same instant, but the stones were beside him.

And God Defied Gravity

He couldn't swim, but the need for air forced his limbs into action. He clawed his way to the surface, gasping and sputtering, much to the amazement and amusement of the others. Ignoring their laughter, he thanked God for sending his angel to save his life by bearing him aside lest he be dashed beneath some stones. From then on he was certain that his Savior was sharing his suffering. He was not alone. His Savior had been leading him the whole time. Though everyone on his team despised him, he had a Friend who would help him through. The marvel was that his God cared enough for him that He would defy gravity to protect him.

With the evidence of the Savior's presence so obvious, Robert thought deeply about his Friend. He regretted again flushing his precious Bible down the drain. How he longed to read from it again. The Word of God would help him rise above the shallow language he heard around him. Possession of a Bible was, of course, strictly forbidden. But, despite the risks, he determined to smuggle another one. Fortunately, he told himself, he would not need to ask his family this time. He could bring it in himself.

CHAPTER 24

Love's Patience Rewarded

Carrying heavy boulders at a quarry eventually strengthened Robert's muscles. But then work was never easy for one as clumsy as he. There was, however, a consolation. Prisoners were allowed to request leave to go home on weekends. Every weekday as he struggled, Robert lived for the weekends.

He looked forward to his next leave, when he could search for a Bible to smuggle into the labor camp. Would he be able to find one? Or had the Red Guards raided his home, discovered the Bibles, and confiscated them?

After the first weekend, he learned the hard way that he couldn't merely request leave and get time off. The guards needed a good reason to grant the permit. While they could be cooperative, it was far easier for them to say no. That way there were fewer chances that they might be reprimanded by their superiors. His request to attend church was flatly denied.

When Robert heard rumors that the kitchen employed the largest staff, he thought, *That would increase my chances of being able to trade shifts with someone. Certainly that would make it easier to go home for the weekends.* Wanting to get Sabbaths off, he applied to be transferred to a kitchen job. To his surprise, the guards granted his request. He quickly discovered that the life of a chef suited him much better.

Love's Patience Rewarded

****

But how to get weekend leave? Permission wasn't automatic. One thing was for certain. Robert's request to take Sabbath off to attend church was consistently rejected. Badly wanting to spend Sabbath with his family and forgetting to trust God again, he once more resorted to the use of deception. And this time he went so far as to devise a code system with the guards in order to be home on the weekend.

When the next weekend arrived, he approached a guard and applied for leave.

"Why do you need to go?" the guard asked.

"I want to visit my girlfriend, who's sick," Robert replied. Actually Mary was well, which was a fact well known to both Robert and the guards. Deceptive though his statement was, it was, in a round-about sort of way, *almost* true; Mary *was* sick. She was in love. As the Song of Solomon says, she was *love sick* (see Song of Solomon 2:5; 5:8). The guards knew he really wanted to attend church but were not allowed to grant him permission for this. Yet they were sympathetic with his situation. When Robert claimed that his girlfriend was ill, they were relieved, because such a situation would provide an acceptable reason for his leave. Writing down that he was nursing a sick girlfriend would keep them from getting into trouble with their superiors, so they granted him permission to go home the next day. By some convoluted logic the guards considered Robert a *true* Christian, and yet conspired with him to *deceive* their superiors so that he could keep the Sabbath. While focusing on being faithful to the fourth commandment, Robert had unfortunately ignored the ninth. Like Jacob, who deceived his father to get the birthright God had promised, Robert deceived the guards to worship God on His holy day. Neither Jacob nor Robert were willing to wait on God to see how He would resolve the problem. Robert had yet to learn lessons from Nicodemus, a Pharisee who wanted to serve Jesus in secret. In time, Nicodemus became known as an Israelite in whom there was no deceit.

The next day Robert presented his leave at the gate and was free to go home and worship God.

At first he traveled by bus when he was on leave, but there were pickpockets on board. Whenever a passenger claimed to have been robbed, the bus stopped and the conductor examined identity cards. Because Robert's card was written in black letters instead of red, conductors knew immediately that Robert was a prisoner and therefore was suspect. Each time, he was taken to the police station for questioning. After being embarrassed this way a few times, Robert considered another mode of transport: a bicycle.

Years of sitting necessitated that he relearn how to ride. Not a few times accidents sent him flying over his handlebars. Crash landings on the pavement were painful, but his determination paid off. Soon he was riding and clanging his bicycle bell like everyone else as he weaved through the stream of cyclists flowing down the city's bicycle lane.

On one of his leaves home, Robert searched his home for a Bible he could smuggle into the labor camp. To his delight he found another English pocket Bible and stuffed it into his underwear. He managed to easily sneak it past the guards and read it at night while the other prisoners were asleep. He slept under a mosquito net every night—even during winter when it was too cold for mosquitoes—because under it he could read with little fear of detection. His only worry was that, when he was granted leave, the guards might find it on his person when he went through check-out.

****

A few months later on one of his leaves, Robert strolled through the park with Mary, and they talked about their past and their future. As it got dark, they headed for his mother's home.

As they sat close together on the living-room couch, Mary, without warning, leaned over and kissed him for the first time. Surprised and joyful, euphoria shot through his system. She kissed him, and it felt good! Yet it was so out of character. Displays of affection are uncommon for Chinese, who prefer to express their love by providing for the other's needs. But she had kissed him. *Mary's love runs very deep,* he thought.

Then Mary looked him in the eye and asked, "When will we get married?"

Caught off guard, Robert was at a loss for words. Yes, he had known they would get married—someday. He had even considered her to be his Rachel because, like Jacob in the Old Testament, Robert and Mary had needed to wait for each other. But wasn't it too soon to talk about marriage? "I haven't been released from hard-labor camp yet," he stammered.

"We're both thirty-five," Mary replied calmly. Definitely, neither one of them was getting any younger. "I know there are many difficulties ahead," Mary continued, "but let's talk it over."

They did. After considerable discussion, they decided to trust in God.

"Why don't we wait until my younger brother is released from hard-labor camp before we marry," Robert suggested. "Then he could join in the wedding."

"Let's ask him," Mary replied.

Robert agreed. "We could arrange to visit him in prison."

So they negotiated with prison authorities. On the appointed day, camp guards escorted Robert and Mary to the visiting area. There seemed to be guards everywhere.

When Robert's younger brother was finally brought out, Robert waited until the guards seemed distracted and said, "We'd really like to have you take part in our wedding. Shall we wait until your release?"

"Don't worry about that," Younger Brother replied. "My heart will be with you." Soon the visitation time ended.

Still Mary's question remained. When *would* they get married? Robert suggested September 29, 1973. "That will be one year and a day after my release from prison."

"Why that date?" Mary asked.

"Do you remember what the psalmist wrote?"

"Tell me," Mary urged. He had her full attention. It seemed she couldn't take her eyes off him.

Gazing back into her eyes, he replied, " 'Weeping may tarry for the night, but joy comes with the morning,' Psalm 30:5." Surely others would ask him why he didn't wait a few days until October 1, China's National Day; but they would not understand the significance of September 28, 1964. The agony of separation ran deep. Robert explained, "By getting married on the twenty-ninth, we will be liberated from that terrible injustice committed against us nine years ago. We'll never forget what happened on September 28, but when that day comes around, we'll look forward to the twenty-ninth!"

Naturally, Mary thought it was wonderful, and she began to prepare. They arranged for a simple wedding.

Before tying the knot, Robert and Mary wanted to make a room for themselves in his mother's house. The materials and labor were not easily obtained. Without connections, little could be accomplished in Shanghai—especially when one wears the "hat" of a counterrevolutionary. In the end they turned to their family and the church members. Together, Elder Sister, Robert's brother-in-law, and some church members helped to prepare the room in a short time. Robert and Mary painted it themselves.

Money was scarce. At the labor camp, Robert earned barely enough for himself to live on. Mary was even worse off because she had lost her job for refusing to work on Sabbath. Robert worried, "With so little income, how can we afford to live, let alone pay for a wedding?"

Under normal circumstances, Robert's financial hardships would have made marriage impractical, if not impossible, but he was *wai kiu.* When Elder Brother heard the news, he offered to send money from California so that they could purchase necessities. He also guaranteed to send the newlyweds a monthly allowance. Elder Sister told them that over the years she had saved several hundred renminbi to help with the cost of the wedding.

Expenses for the newlyweds' nest were kept to a minimum, too. Almost all the furniture they bought for their room was secondhand. Robert remembered the stories about the Adventist pioneers and especially the story of the wedding of James and Ellen White. Things were simpler in those days. They didn't know about many of the appliances available these days—yet they survived. Robert and Mary didn't have much in the way of earthly goods, but they did love each other. With that they were content.

To cut costs, Mary decided not to wear the traditional red wedding attire made of silk and covered with embroidery. Nor did she wear the traditional Western wedding gown. Instead, the couple purchased sets of new Sun Yat-sen jackets for the event.

They didn't buy expensive presents for each other either, nor did they ask friends and relatives to bring gifts. No one could have afforded them anyway. Gold—the most common gift at weddings—was extremely difficult to come by in Liberated China. Wedding bands were unnecessary, because they not only couldn't afford them but also believed their love was sealed by the cross of Christ.

With the wedding date set, Robert's time away from the labor camp passed more quickly, while his days laboring in the industrial center dragged endlessly. Instead of lying in bed under his mosquito net reading his Bible as had been his custom, Robert thought about Mary. He longed to do something special for her. Eventually, he decided to fashion a wedding souvenir. Taking two plastic badges from the Cultural Revolution, he refashioned them.

One heart-shaped badge was red with a picture of Chairman Mao. In it was engraved the Chinese characters for "loyalty" and "faithfulness." Thinking it perfect for lovers, Robert removed the picture of Chairman Mao and replaced it with one of Jesus. The other badge was more nondescript. Using a drop of his own blood from a finger, he drew a heart on it. Then he carefully smeared a large red cross over the heart. The points of it extended beyond the heart. Cutting a mini-photo of himself and Mary into the shape of a heart, he placed it in the center of the heart. Below he quoted 1 Corinthians 13:8, which says, "Love never fails."

Looking at the finished product, he realized that it seemed clumsy. Certainly, he thought, he could never be an artist. Nevertheless, it was the best he could do. Mary would love it because it meant he had been thinking of her. As ill-fashioned as his gift was, he eagerly waited to see the surprised look on her face when he would present it to her on their wedding day.

When the time neared, Robert requested and obtained leave to attend his wedding. Because the wedding was to take place around Liberation Day, China's second biggest holiday, the guards granted him the national holiday, the day of rest, and three days for the marriage. It added up to nine days off to be with his bride!

Not all was rosy, though. Shortly before the actual event, the couple received a police warning: "Invite no guests to your wedding."

Clearly the police feared it might become a counterrevolutionary party. Not wanting any problems on their special day, Robert and Mary took the warning seriously. Invitations were kept to family members only. One was sent to Mary's father, who was still required to "learn from the peasants" in Anwi province. Another was sent to Robert's younger brother even though they knew the hard-labor farm would not let him come.

The actual wedding day was almost like any other day. All Adventist churches were still closed in 1973. The Three-Self Church would not marry them under their roof because Robert was a counterrevolutionary. Considering the circumstances, he and Mary chose to be registered with the local government.

Dressed in their new clothes, they walked to the Public Security Bureau. Outside they waited for Mary's father, who had been granted permission to attend the wedding. When he didn't arrive at the appointed time, Robert and Mary stepped inside.

They stood before the registrar, awaiting his blessing. In a matter of minutes, they were husband and wife.

Marriage certificate in hand, Robert escorted Mary home. They sang and prayed together in the living room and dedicated their lives to the Lord. No one was there to share the moment with them.

They opened no gifts because they had requested none. Instead, they exchanged cards. Robert had written a poem for the occasion in his. On Mary's card was a picture of a basket full of fruit. Beneath the basket were some Bible verses relating to fruit.

Their quiet peace was interrupted by an impervious knocking. Thinking it might be Mary's father arriving from Anwi, they answered the door.

There stood a police officer in uniform.

Stepping inside, the uninvited guest snooped around their new home, asked Robert some mundane questions, and offered some advice and information that he thought Robert should know. Then he left.

After regaining their composure, the newlyweds examined their mail. Robert's American brother had sent a telegram and a beautiful wedding card from California.

Suddenly Robert remembered his souvenir. "I've got a surprise for you," Robert announced.

"You do! For me?" exclaimed Mary. "You shouldn't have."

"I made it myself," Robert replied. "It's a souvenir."

Love's Patience Rewarded

"That reminds me," Mary said. "I almost forgot your gift."

"What have you got for me?" Robert asked.

"Secret!" Mary teased. "If I told you, it wouldn't be a surprise."

"Let me present you with mine first," Robert suggested.

"No, I've got it handy. I can easily give it to you now," Mary said.

Not wanting to appear greedy, Robert urged, "No, Mary, please take mine first."

Mary politely refused, and Robert graciously assented. Immediately she pulled out two cushions with nylon covers. "They're prayer pillows," she explained. "Read the verses," she urged. One read, "Rejoicing in hope, patient in tribulation, continuing in prayer. Romans 12:12." On the other pillow was a verse from Revelation 8: "The smoke of the incense from the prayers of the saints, ascended up before God out of the angel's hand." As Robert looked at the workmanship, he felt humbled. These were souvenirs he would treasure forever. Then he remembered his gift. How could he present her with the work of his unskilled labor? By comparison, it seemed so inadequate. Mary's pillows were works of art, he thought. But he could never become a craftsman.

"Now what do you have for me?" Mary asked shyly.

Reluctantly taking out his redesigned badges, he presented them to her. When she saw the hearts, the cross, their photos and the picture of Jesus, she was visibly touched. Clearly she would value his presents also. For some women, it seemed, a labor of love was more meaningful than a work of art!

As it grew dark outside, the two prepared for their first night together. Looking around them, they were reminded that they possessed few material goods. From a worldly point of view, their life was a failure. Their clothes were shabby and their home simple, but all that mattered little. They had Jesus in the home, Robert thought, which made the family happy. What did they really lack? Nothing important. Their love for each other and for their Savior filled all their needs.

****

Not long after the wedding, Mary's father arrived from Anwi province. Apologizing profusely, he explained, "The guards at the labor farm delayed granting my permit to leave until the last minute. I came as quickly as I could, but catching both the boat and the train in such a short time was impossible." Unspoken was the idea that perhaps the authorities had wanted him to miss the wedding.

That night they celebrated his arrival at a Muslim restaurant and had a small wedding feast with all the family members who were able to attend.

Though they couldn't go on a real honeymoon, Robert and Mary traveled to some scenic areas around Shanghai. When they checked into a hotel, Robert showed their new marriage license because, being a prisoner, he lacked a proper ID. His only identification was "in" or "out" permits for prisoners in hard-labor camps. Having to use the marriage certificate to register at a hotel reminded him that even in marriage, they would remain separated. He tried to enjoy every minute he had with his new bride.

All too soon, however, he had to return to the labor camp, never knowing when he would be granted a leave again. Whenever he *was* allowed to visit Mary, time flew like the wind. Back in the prison, time seemed to stop entirely. Sadly, there would be many a time when Robert was forced to remain in the labor camp and spend weekends and holidays in sorrow and longing.

There was nothing he could do about it except pray for an early release. And pray he did.

CHAPTER 25

A Dream Come True

The inmates considered Robert slightly strange because he slept under his mosquito net all year long. The others set up their nets in the summer when the mosquitoes were numerous but took them down in the winter. They could not figure out why Robert never took his net down. As far as Robert was concerned, it was a good thing.

After smuggling a pocket English Bible into the hard labor camp, he wanted to read it undetected. The net served to veil his activities. Early in the morning or late at night, when the light was dim, he could take his Bible out from its hiding place under his pillow and read it.

The fact that it was written in English was advantageous because none of his roommates could read English. If it were discovered, no one would know it was a Bible. Nevertheless, in an effort to avoid trouble, Robert read when the room was empty, or whenever he felt certain his roommates were asleep. He had to make sure that no one observed him reading it. Any witness could report him to the authorities. In actual fact, however, he seldom read for very long. At the end of the day, he was weary to the bone. Work in the camp was hard. Every night, when he returned from his assigned duties, he felt fatigued. His Bible was what kept him going. Without it, his physical exhaustion would have rubbed off on his spiritual life. Reading portions of the Bible every night recharged him and made it easier for him to struggle through another day in the camp.

When he was granted leave to visit Mary, Robert dared not leave his Bible behind. As he could never be sure whether or not his bed might be searched by guards or roommates, he took his Bible home with him. This necessitated smuggling the book in and out of the camp repeatedly. Fortunately, doing so was not as dangerous as it had been in the detention centers. In the labor camp, no one searched bars of soap for needles. Instead, the guards studied each prisoner carefully. If anything seemed suspicious, the inmate might be frisked. Never, as far as Robert had been able to observe, did the guards rifle through bags.

Robert wrapped his Bible in a cloth and placed it in his bag. For months his bag was never inspected.

Then one winter, as he was lining up to take leave, Robert noticed that the guards were inspecting all the bags. Fear gripped him. What were they searching for? Had someone reported having a watch stolen? He couldn't remember any such announcement. The only thing he could think about was his Bible. Had one of his twenty cellmates observed him reading it and reported him? There was nothing he could do. If he got out of line, he would raise the guard's suspicion. It would give them reason to frisk him or search his bag. The last thing he wanted was to have his precious Bible confiscated. He dared not think about the consequences if it were found. He felt he was suffering enough working in the labor camp. He did not wish to have torture added to his schedule. So he remained in line, hoping the guards would find what they were seeking before they came to him.

Suddenly, he felt a funny feeling as something inside his pants pressed against him. Smiling, he realized it was his Bible! He had forgotten to put it in his bag. It was hidden in his underwear. Robert thought to himself, *God knows everything. He knew about the inspection today and caused me to hide my Bible in a different location today.* Inwardly, he praised God for His infinite wisdom.

Nervous though he was, when it was his turn in line, Robert walked confidently up to the guard, who opened Robert's bag and found nothing suspicious inside. Once outside the labor camp, Robert breathed easier.

A Dream Come True

When he arrived home, he politely knocked on the door. Mary opened it, and Robert announced, "The Lord wrought a miracle for me today!" He told her about the guard's inspection and how he had gotten the Bible home safely. "God really preserved this precious little Bible for me. Once again He saved me from undue punishment."

****

Weeks passed. The days blurred together into a bleak sameness. Then came a day Robert would never forget, a day that proved to him that God was nearer than he thought.

That cold night, as Robert walked back to his dorm room after finishing his duties at the labor camp, he felt tired and hungry and cold and miserable. With each weary step toward the dreary dorm, the distance seemed to increase. The future flashed before Robert, and it seemed long and dark. Under the stars, he walked alone to the room. The other prisoners had gone to the mess hall to eat, but Robert had not joined them because he knew that the food was prepared in lard.

When he arrived in his barren room, he addressed his hunger by pouring a cup of water, stirring in some sugar, and drinking it. He was alone, so he knelt by his bunk and prayed silently.

Crawling inside his mosquito net, he flopped onto his bed and fell into a deep sleep.

Suddenly, his sleep was interrupted by an uncontrollable urge to visit the bathroom, which was outside. Leaving the dormitory, he strolled to the smelly outhouse and addressed his need, and then returned to his bed and, with the aid of moonlight, looked at the time on his watch. Night would soon streak into dawn. Unable to go back to sleep, he lay on his bunk and contemplated a dream he had just had.

In the dream, he was helping people put out a fire. He had been afraid that some sparks might have been missed, so he had run to grab another bucket of water. When he returned to the scene, a few sparks were still flying, which he doused with the contents in his bucket. Then in the dream someone whose Chinese name meant "moisten the people" walked up to him, thanked him, and shook his hand.

What could the dream mean? Robert wondered. *How would the Freudian psychoanalysts interpret it?*

Dreams are the culmination of the day's activities. Why had he dreamed about a fire? Then he recalled that he had been on leave the day before. Early in the morning, when he had stepped on the ferry that would take him toward the labor camp, the sky had grown dark and cloudy. Waves in the river beat relentlessly against the side of the ferry. Just then it seemed he had heard a voice whisper into his ear. What was the verse?

Reaching under his pillow, he pulled his pocket English Bible out from its hiding place and opened to the verse. Squinting to focus in the dim morning light, he read, "O Israel, fear not for I have redeemed thee. I have called thee by thy name, thou art mine. When thou passest through the waters, I will be with thee, and through the rivers, they shall not overflow thee; when thou walkest through the fire thou shall not be burned; neither shall the flame kindle upon thee. For I am the Lord thy God." Having heard the words at the time, and having read them again in his cot, Robert was comforted. No matter how dark his future appeared, his name was known to the God of heaven.

As his thoughts returned to the events of the previous morning, Robert unconsciously slipped his Bible back under his pillow. It would be safe there because no one would see it. He recalled that while he was on a bus, he had seen a fire engine lying on its side in a field. He thought to himself that those suffering in the fire had placed their hope in the fire engine, but it had failed them. Man's help is so limited. Often, as in the case of this unfortunate fire truck, it is in vain. As he pictured it again, another verse came him. "Whence cometh my help? My help cometh from the Lord!"

Suddenly, Robert saw flames burst out beside him and heard them crackle loudly. His mosquito net had caught fire. In seconds the flames spread. "Fire!" he called and sprang out of bed.

The inmate in the bunk above him jumped down. Together they fought the flames.

Soon the others were awake also. Gathering around, they asked, "What happened?" and "Why?"

A Dream Come True

No one seemed to know the answers. The one who had carelessly dropped the match after lighting a cigarette knew, but he wasn't talking.

The event was very meaningful to both Robert and his cellmates. "This is the first time something like this has happened in years!" they exclaimed. Because the fire had started so near Robert's bed, everything around him could have easily burned. Had he slept, he tried not to imagine what might have happened.

His life and the lives of his roommates had been spared from an inferno because of his dream about a fire. Was it coincidence or providence?

Robert was convinced that psychology alone could not explain his dream. Seeing the fire truck on its side might have triggered it, but psychology cannot explain why the fire occurred moments after the dream. Robert believed God had sent him the dream to protect him. His pocket Bible played its part in saving his life, too. Had he not pulled it out to read, he might easily have drifted back to sleep before the fire erupted. The dream was evidence that God was present in the Godforsaken labor camp. Like Jacob, who dreamed about the ladder of angels, Robert exclaimed to himself, "Surely God is in this camp, and I forgot." His being saved from the fire renewed both his faith and his strength. Knowing that God was near helped him perform his duties better.

On his next leave, the first thing Robert said to Mary when he stepped through the door was, "God performed another miracle for me in the camp this week! This one is even more remarkable than the last."

After he had shared the story with her, they sang songs of praise and thanksgiving, and then prayed, thanking God for delivering him from the fire.

CHAPTER 26

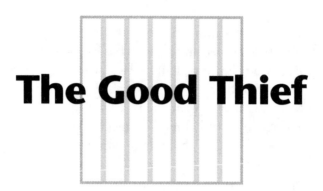

The Good Thief

After experiencing three miracles in the labor camp, Robert's spiritual courage increased. Having been fearful to talk about his faith for so long, he gradually crawled out of his shell. Looking around the labor camp, he considered each prisoner. Most of them behaved so crudely, they would have made a hardened sailor feel uncomfortable. One young man on the quarry team, Luk Tin Shing, seemed different. Although he had been arrested for stealing, he was no common hustler.

Robert tried to get to know him better. Little by little he discovered that life had dealt the young thief many hardships. His mother had died while he was imprisoned the first time. His only remaining relative was his aging father, who, at 88, was handicapped. There was something about Luk Tin Shing that made him different from most of the other prisoners in the industrial center. Robert felt that this thief actually possessed some redeeming qualities. He didn't smoke or drink, and he was industrious. Often he brought his father's soiled clothing from home and, in his spare time, washed it and then dried it in front of the furnace. Robert also observed that he visited his co-workers when they were sick in the hospital.

He liked the thief so much that he traveled with him on foot whenever they were granted leave on the same day. Robert took advantage of the situation to share Bible stories and proverbs with him. He even gave him some money, some clothes, and entertained him in his home. Luk Tin Shing expressed great appreciation.

On one of their leaves, the young thief told Robert that there had been a fire in his father's home. Robert gave him some money to fix up the house. Jokingly, Robert said one day, "You're too good of a man to remain single. I'm going to look for a nice young lady for you!" Although they laughed at the comment, Robert seriously looked for a young woman for him, and then decided that, because his friend was not a Christian, he could not introduce him to a church member.

On one leave, they noticed an old blind woman who was lost. They took her to her bus and accompanied her to her home. Robert was glad to see how zealous the young thief was to go the second mile to help others.

After dropping the elderly woman off at her home, Robert and Luk Tin Shing set off for Robert's house. As they strode down the sidewalk, Robert said, "I like poems."

"Me too," said the thief.

Grateful to have found a kindred spirit, Robert added, "I compose them continually."

"Me too!" The young thief smiled.

Suddenly Robert felt an urge to say, "The Bible is precious to me."

Without batting an eye, Luk replied, "Could you lend me a copy to read?" At the time, very few Bibles were available. Owning one was dangerous, and lending one was perilous. In spite of that, Robert decided to try. When they arrived at his home, he searched everywhere until he discovered a pocket Chinese New Testament, some Bible correspondence lessons, and a few religious books. Among them were Chinese translations of *Paradise Lost* and *Paradise Regained*. As he lent the rare books to his friend, he said, "These are precious to me. Be very careful with them in the labor camp. If you're caught with them, they'll be confiscated, and you will be in trouble, and so will I."

Luk agreed. With a smile, he promised, "I'll read them, copy my favorite paragraphs, and return them."

He read the books secretly. On their next leave together, he handed Robert an envelope. In it was a note thanking Robert for giving him the money and for sharing the books. "I accept the truth," the note read. "Once I was lonely and wanted to destroy myself. Now I am happy." A tear welled up in Robert's eye as he read. He felt certain that God had wanted him to work in the labor camp to meet this good-hearted thief.

Not long after this, an inmate told Robert that Luk Tin Shing was in the labor camp's guardhouse. Frightened, Robert wondered what the matter was. Had their friendship been discovered?

A couple of days later, Robert was surprised and delighted to learn that both he and the thief would be granted leave for Western New Year. How eagerly he anticipated that holiday! It would be the first New Year's Day since his wedding. He had been married for only a couple of months and longed to be with his wife. The news made the next few weeks pass quickly.

A few days before his leave, Robert dashed over to the police office to get his permit. When he stepped inside, a guard immediately announced, "You must remain here, contemplate your problem, and give an account of your guilt!" The words hit Robert like cold water splashed in his face.

"Why? What?" he stammered, hoping for some sort of hint.

The guard answered stiffly, "You think it over yourself."

Having not the slightest clue as to what he might have done wrong, Robert remained in the police station for half an hour seeking information, but received none. "I think you know," was all the guard would say. Exasperated, Robert asked, "May I send a message to my family? Because they're expecting me, they'll be worried when I don't show up."

"Unnecessary!" the guard answered coldly.

Disappointed about having to spend New Year's separated from Mary, Robert dragged his feet all the way to the dormitory. Because his friend was being held in the guardhouse, Robert reasoned that his guilt was somehow entangled with the thief's. It did not necessarily mean that the thief had reported him to the police. Perhaps it meant that he had committed his life to God and it had become apparent. If that were the case, then all his things would have been checked thoroughly and the books he had borrowed from Robert would have been discovered and confiscated. For preaching the gospel, Robert reflected, he had already spent eight years in prison. He wore a "counterrevolutionary hat." Praying to God and preaching the gospel in the detention center had resulted in his being sent to a hard-labor camp. Besides all that, the government would surely consider him as guilty as the thief. How much additional punishment that might mean, Robert feared to calculate.

Soon after that gloomy day, another guard called Robert into his office, "You have recommitted a crime," he said. Evidently, the guards knew that Robert was ignorant of his friend's crime.

Robert felt that he should say something. Quietly he confessed, "I often exhorted him to escape from sin." The guard seemed surprised. Robert added in self-defense, "I could soon see that my efforts were useless."

The guard sneered, "He can defend himself, but you are charged with your own problem." Then, in a patronizing tone, he explained, "In this labor camp we reform prisoners by Marxist principles and Mao Zedong thought, while you want to use the Bible to reform them. You are anti-Marxist and anti-Communist. More to the point, you are against our policy of reformation."

It was true, Robert thought. Experience had shown him that people could only be reformed by the saving grace of Jesus Christ. Without God's spirit, human reformation plans are futile. Any character development is enabled through Him. Wisdom told him to keep his opinions to himself.

Seeing that Robert had nothing more to say, the guard continued. "As punishment, you are not permitted to spend Chinese New Year with your bride of three months. Instead, you must stay in camp for three months without leave."

Initially, Robert thought his punishment was more than he could bear. It was as if a dart had struck him in the heart.

For the next few months, Robert worked his regular shift. In the evening, weary from the day's tasks, he was called to the guard's office to report everything that had happened between himself and the former thief. Because he did not know what to report, he was forced to remain in the office and think about his crime. To ensure that he did not escape or attempt to send a letter secretly, a guard followed his every step.

Once, Mary and Elder Sister came to visit him. They brought food but went away disappointed. He heard the guard yell, "You are prohibited from meeting with him. Go back home!" Robert worried that the authorities might harm his family. When he learned that they had indeed ordered an investigation, he feared the police would search his house. Then they would find more of his precious books.

As the days dragged into months, the nights became unbearable. Robert tossed and turned, wondering what to report. Repeatedly he asked himself, "Did I make a mistake?"

Initially, he thought not.

Then he asked himself, "What if Luk Tin Shing had recanted his faith, or worse, been caught stealing again?"

Ultimately, he concluded that he had made a mistake. For giving ready credence to a young man whom he did not completely understand, Robert decided he was to blame. Sowing the seed of the gospel is a dangerous job that requires great self-sacrifice. From a human perspective, it is often viewed as a wasteful work. Judas certainly thought so when he smelled the costly perfume Mary poured on Jesus' feet. On many sleepless nights, Robert reflected that most of the human race has rejected God's offer of eternal life; nevertheless, Jesus died that all might be saved. Much of His blood, though shed in love, was spilled in vain. One can never be certain what will happen to the seed once sown, yet, to mix metaphors, the Bible cautions against throwing pearls before swine. Perhaps, Robert thought, he had fed his pearls to a pig unawares.

The next evening, he added to his confession, "There was once a man named William Miller who said, 'I had wrongs, but in charity.' So it is with me!" Rather than confess that the gospel was wrong, Robert admitted, "My preaching was imperfect. I sowed seed that may have fallen on stony ground. Had my love for my friend been in knowledge and good judgment, perhaps the seed would not have been wasted. For that, I blame myself. My only hope is that someday he will repent of his crimes and sins before God and man."

As the days passed, when Robert wasn't working or meditating on his crime, Mary was in his thoughts. He missed her terribly. At times it seemed he would never see her again.

Soon Chinese New Year arrived. Other prisoners were granted leave to celebrate the holiday. As they received their permits, Robert pined to see all the members of his extended family, who would come to his

The Good Thief

home on Chinese New Year's Eve. He longed to be with his wife and aging mother on that special day. But it was not to be. While his family was united in his home, he spent the night inside the walls of the labor camp. Through his suffering, Robert tried to console himself with the thought that Jesus and his Heavenly Father suffered separation that humanity might one day be reunited with Him forever. There he could celebrate an uninterrupted communion with his loved ones.

Three months later an officer from the Public Safety Bureau called Robert into his office for questioning. After Robert again admitted his crime, the officer said, "In New China we don't use Christianity to reform prisoners. Instead we use Marxism and Mao Zedong thought."

Reading between the lines, Robert guessed that the former thief had not recanted as he had once feared. Was his punishment due to jealousy? The guards had seen that Christ had succeeded where Marx had failed, but they could not admit that the power of Jesus changes lives.

"Ordinarily," the guard continued, "we'd extend your sentence for your crimes. But you're a good man. You're concerned about the reformation of criminals. For this, we commend you. It's a shame you weren't born in another place and time. If you had been, you might've been good for China. Leave the old ways behind and use our methods."

With that, Robert was told that he was again free to apply for weekend and holiday leaves. However, as he dismissed him, the guard added a final caveat, "I'm letting you off with a warning this time. Be aware that we will watch your every move."

It proved to be a promise well kept.

CHAPTER 27

An American Visits China

In 1972, American President Richard M. Nixon was politically isolated at home by his enemies in the State Department, due to accusations surrounding the Watergate Scandal, as well as by vicious media bent on proving that a Republican president who perjures himself while in office will face dire consequences. Hoping to put Watergate behind him, Nixon conducted a whirlwind tour of personal diplomacy, visiting the Soviet Union, the Middle East, and what was then called Communist China.

In his meetings with Chairman Mao and Premier Chou En-lai, Nixon permanently altered China's relationship with America. Until Nixon's overture, the door to the West was shut. But in the decade following Nixon's visit, the door as at least ajar. Selected, determined individuals could squeeze through that door into China. One of those individuals was John Huang, Robert's elder brother, a neurosurgeon based in California who had emigrated to the United States shortly after Liberation. In 1975 he requested a visa. His only wish was to visit his family in Shanghai after being separated from them for more than twenty years.

Getting a visa, however, did not prove easy. His application hit one obstacle after another. Two years of perseverance and determination paid off. Excited, with visa in hand, he wrote Robert a letter.

An American Visits China

In 1977, a guard approached Robert with that letter in his hand. "A rare event is about to occur in New China," the guard gruffly informed Robert. "An American wants to visit his motherland." Robert didn't understand where the conversation was heading. "You're a very lucky man, Criminal 1068." The guard handed Robert the letter. "Your letter says your brother will fly all the way from California to Shanghai just to meet you and your family. Arrangements have been made. When he comes, we'll take you out of prison and drive you to the appointed place. You are to say nothing that will shame your country. Is that understood?"

Robert said he did.

The guard smiled broadly. "If you say anything contrary to the socialist's road, you alone will be responsible for the consequences."

When the guard left, Robert tore open the letter and read it. His brother planned to arrive in the fruitful, golden fall, Shanghai's finest season. As the time neared, suspense mounted. Robert checked the mail daily in hope of a letter or telegram. At last one came. Robert's brother was the head of a touring party that would be coming from an undisclosed city, it said.

Robert prepared as best he could for his brother's arrival. He had his hair cut, purchased a honeydew melon, a rare delicacy in Shanghai, and wrote a poem to accompany it. Since his brother would arrive during Liberation Day, one of China's biggest holidays, Robert could count on a two-day leave, which he requested and was granted.

On the morning of October 2, Robert could hardly wait to go to the railway station, where he would be allowed to board the train to meet his brother. Shanghai had changed so much since he and his brother had taken separate paths, Robert reflected. What different lives they had led in the past three decades. His brother had become a successful doctor in the West, while he had remained behind to become an impoverished prisoner of conscience.

With permit in hand, Robert left the industrial center that formed his labor camp and headed home. Once there, he went up to his bedroom and began performing his last chore—pressing his clothes.

Suddenly there was a knock on the door. A police officer entered the living room, gave a few words of explanation to the family, and then called Robert outside. "We want to have a short talk with you in the police station," was all he would say.

Despite the fact that he suspected it was a trick, Robert did not object. He knew his only choice was to accompany the officer. Hoping that the officer only wished to caution him and instruct him before he met his brother, Robert remained cheery. But as each step took them nearer to the station, his hopes faded. The guard kept close watch of him, especially in crowded areas. With the railway station in sight, the lie became transparent when the guard said, "Your brother is waiting for you at the police station and will talk to you there."

Guessing that the police feared he might escape if they let him board the train, Robert said nothing. Irritated by Robert's silence, the guard watched him more closely. Did he expect him to bolt for the train?

Outside the police station, Robert noticed an additional bad sign—a jeep with two labor-camp guards, one in plain clothes. As Robert and the officer approached the jeep, one of the guards asked in mock surprise, "Why didn't you return for duty?"

Surely they knew that his permit was still valid. They knew he had permission to see his American brother, who was supposed to be waiting for him at the station. Did the authorities have other plans? It seemed they needed an excuse to call him in for questioning. He protested, to no avail.

Together the guards escorted Robert into the police station. For half an hour they listened to Robert's pleas, explanations, and attempts to defend himself, and then cut him off.

"Don't waste your time talking," they announced gruffly. "We're fed up with you. Come now and take the consequences!"

Having seen a pair of handcuffs in the pocket of a guard, Robert guessed the worst. Waving away his request to call his family, they hustled Robert into the jeep and sped off. With any hope of seeing his brother completely dashed, Robert was heartbroken.

Back in the camp, Robert was shut indoors under guard, with the added warning, "When we let you out, don't go anywhere near the main gate!"

He was allowed to perform his duties the next day. Rumors spread that he had committed a crime while on leave and had had to be forced back. Many eyed him suspiciously.

Later, Robert learned that his brother stayed in Shanghai with his family for three days. Although they spent weary hours calling and visiting government officials, it was a waste of time. No one was allowed to communicate with Robert by any means. Keenly disappointed, they had eventually given up. His brother left the city on schedule. Throughout Dr. John Huang's stay in China, Robert remained confined.

For almost a month, all of Robert's requests for leave were denied. Then to his joy, he was given a permit to go home briefly. Before he walked through the gate, a guard explained, "Because you're a counterrevolutionary and your elder brother is now a foreigner, the commanding officer decided it was too dangerous for you to contact each other."

Hearing the explanation made Robert's stomach turn, but he said nothing. As his brother had already departed, protesting wouldn't change anything. Thinking of Mary instead, he stepped through the gate and headed home.

In bed beside Mary that night, Robert prayed, "God, I don't understand why You allowed the government to be so cruel to my family. Nevertheless, I consent to Your will for my family and for myself. Surely there is a reason for what just happened that I will comprehend later." The line of a hymn came to his mind. "Have Thine own way, Lord, have Thine own way. Thou art the Potter, I am the clay."

He knew that, despite the hardships, God was with him in the hard labor camp. Hadn't God made it clear in the quarry? Hadn't He shown His Presence the night he dreamed about the fire? Perhaps, like Job, he didn't need to understand everything. Accepting that God was in control was enough.

He reminded himself that Jesus told His disciples the day would come when they would carry their own crosses. In this world, suffering was part of the Christian life. Looking back over the years, Robert saw how God had sustained him through his prison trials despite his own lack of faith. Surely God, who knew the end from the beginning, had a plan for him now of which he knew nothing.

Indeed He did, and it was beyond Robert's wildest imagination.

Epilogue

With God, the Future's So Bright, It's Blinding

Many changes took place in China after the death of Chairman Mao in 1976. China went through four turbulent years under the rule of Mao Zedong's widow and the notorious Gang of Four. By the end of the decade, Deng Xiao Ping rose to power as the leader of the Party. Being reform minded, he wanted to right wrongs and help China to enter the world stage.

High on Deng's agenda was prison reform. Soon Robert learned that he and his younger brother could appeal their cases. Because his younger brother was a Christian medical doctor, during the Cultural Revolution he had two marks against him; one for being Christian and another for practicing medicine. Robert's case was simpler because he was just a pastor. Robert decided to help his younger brother with his appeal before working on his own. After his younger brother was released, Robert made his own appeal and his case was cleared in early 1979. In time the government not only reinstated his full citizenship but also reissued his ministerial license—a remarkable thing for one imprisoned as a counterrevolutionary.

Dr. John Huang, Robert's elder brother in California, came to a conviction because of his trip to Shanghai. It convinced him to help his relatives emigrate to the United States. Because Robert's father was an American citizen and his brother lived in California, he qualified for immigration—provided he had a sponsor. Later in 1979, Elder Brother offered to sponsor not only Robert but the whole family. As a successful neurosurgeon, he had the means to support them.

When the sponsorship papers arrived, Robert and six other members of his immediate family, including Mary and his younger brother, traveled to the newly opened American embassy in Beijing. There they were issued immigrant visas.

Robert lived and worked in the United States for several years, often telling about his experience working as a pastor in Shanghai's underground church. Eventually, he obtained a doctorate from Andrews University. For his dissertation, he researched methods to evangelize Chinese.

After receiving his degree, Robert was hired to work with Adventist church members in China. At the time of this writing, his office is in Hong Kong. From there, he travels the world as a representative of Chinese Christians both in China and wherever Chinese can be found.

Today Robert is grateful that God gave him an opportunity to witness for Him in a time when Adventism almost died in China. He praises God that a guard's prediction proved false. The prison floor did not rot beneath him. As he looks back over his life, he feels that, dark though it seemed at the time, his Savior led him every step of the way. Prison life taught him the value of time. Since his release, he has spent every day trying to be a blessing to someone and striving to lead another Chinese to Christ.

More books by Stanley Maxwell and others:

The Man Who Couldn't Be Killed
Stanley Maxwell
An unforgettable story of faith and miraculous deliverance in Communist China at the height of the Cultural Revolution. Mr. Wong's unflinching courage and the miracles that saved his life will inspire you to believe in God who is greater that any problem.
0816312354. Paperback.
US$10.99, Can$16.49.

The Man Who Lived Twice
Stanley Maxwell
From a re-education camp in Communist Vietnam, where torture often challenges faith, comes a compelling story of one man's conviction and miraculous deliverance. Stanley Maxwell, author of *The Man Who Couldn't Be Killed* brings us another story of witness through trial that will inspire you to treasure your freedoms and to stand up for your faith.
0816313725. Paperback.
US$10.99, Can$16.49.

Under the Shadow of the Rising Sun
Donald and Vesta West Mansell
A missionary family en route to Africa gets caught in the Japanese occupation of the Philippines and spends three years in a prisoner of war camp. A powerful true story of survival and faith during the second world war.
0-8163-1976-6. Paperback.
US$14.99, Can$22.49.

Order from your ABC by calling **1-800-765-6955**, or get online and shop our virtual store at **www.AdventistBookCenter.com**.
- Read a chapter from your favorite book
- Order online
- Sign up for email notices on new products

Prices subject to change without notice.